Political Change in Europe

The Left and the Future of the Atlantic Alliance

Edited by DOUGLAS EDEN

and F.E. SHORT

BASIL BLACKWELL · OXFORD

First published in 1980 by Basil Blackwell Publisher, Oxford in association with the Institute for European Studies.

British Library Cataloguing in Publication Data

Political change in Europe.
  1. Europe − Foreign relations − United States
  2. United States − Foreign relations − Europe
  3. Europe − Foreign relations − 1945-
  4. United States − Foreign relations − 1945-
  5. Communist parties
  I. Eden, Douglas   II. Short, Frederick
  327.4′073   D1065.U5

ISBN 0-631-12525-6

Typeset by Getset, Eynsham
Printed in Great Britain
by Book Plan Limited, Worcester

Political Change
in Europe

Contents

Preface

Contributors

1 The European Left: An Historical Perspective
   HUGH THOMAS   1

2 British Labour and the West
   STEPHEN HASELER   15

3 The British Left, Trade Unions and Democracy
   PAUL JOHNSON   30

4 Italian Political Parties and Italian Society
   ARRIGO LEVI   43

5 The Crisis of the Italian Political System and the
   Elections of June 1979
   GIUSEPPE ARE   63

6 The Communist Party and the Union of the Left
   in France
   PHILIP NATAS   81

7 The West German Social Democratic Party
   PAUL FRIEDRICH   93

8 Trends in the Scandinavian Left
   DAVID GRESS   101

9 Europe and America
   LUIGI BARZINI   125

10 America and Europe
   DAVID BOWEN   134

11 American Opinions and Perceptions of Political
   Change in Europe
   ROY GODSON   143

12 The Alliance under Stress: National Interests
   and Political Change
   DOUGLAS EDEN   148

   Index   161

Preface

Western Europe remains one of the major pillars supporting the edifice of the Western world. Against a background of growing Soviet power and reach, recent world events – particularly in Southwest Asia and the Middle East have brought into the open some of the underlying tensions between the nations of Western Europe and the ultimate guarantor of Western security, the United States. Yet, these tensions, which reflect marginal differences of perspective and interest between various members of the Atlantic alliance, are unlikely to develop of themselves into serious schisms.

In the long run, the threat to the unity of the Western alliance lies in the *ideological* and *political* battle which is being waged within the borders of some member countries. The United States remains essentially consensual. The ideological and political clash is most acute in the nations of Western Europe, and it is most palpable in the parties and movements of the European Left where political change is occurring and posing a potential threat to the community of interest and values of the democratic world.

The communist parties of Southern Europe are powerful actors on the European political stage and the phenomenon popularly known as 'Eurocommunism' presents formidable intellectual and political challenges to democrats. Communist parties, whether 'Eurocommunist' or 'neo-Stalinist', whether in or out of political office, present a serious threat to the cohesion of the alliance.

Developments within the social democratic parties of Northern Europe also give cause for concern. For instance, the British Labour Party has recently sought to open a dialogue with the communist parties of Southern Europe. Trends within the labour movements, principally the trade unions, of Western Europe have important implications for the whole direction of European politics.

Since the Second World War, Western Europe has been blessed with parties of the Left whose traditions have placed them firmly in the Western camp. Indeed, the West German SPD, the British Labour party and some of the socialist and social democratic parties in other European countries have a more reliable 'Atlanticist' record than some of Europe's conservative parties and elites, as Professor Thomas and Dr Haseler point out in the first two chapters.

On the Left today, the debate is rather different. It is suffused with all kinds of dangerous impulses − notions of neutralism between East and West, pliant attitudes towards the Soviet Union, visceral antagonisms towards the mixed economy − which could wholly transform the internal politics and the geopolitical perspectives of key Western nations.

Consequently, an understanding of political change on the Left in Western Europe is essential for anyone concerned with the future health and stability of the Western position in the world. American attitudes to such change, both at elite and public levels, also need to be understood.

We hope this book will contribute to that understanding. It consists of assessments about political change in Western Europe, and some of its implications, by scholars from most of the Western European nations. The contributors come from various political backgrounds.

Their essays tend to be pitched at the level of a study of political parties (their strengths and influence, debates within them, factional trends) rather than at the level of philosophical and speculative controversy. There is an emphasis on Britain and Italy which, arguably, are the major European nations most vulnerable to internal political change.

In order to set these essays on the European Left in a broader, Western, context, we also present two short essays by American observers of political change in Europe, one a Congressman, the other a Professor. In turn, Luigi Barzini makes some observations from Europe about the United States.

The concluding chapter attempts to draw the various themes together, relating national interests, government policies and superpower influences to political change in Europe and its implications for the Atlantic alliance.

We would like to thank Dr Stephen Haseler for supervising so much of the work involved in putting this book together and Mr Ronald Halliday for his editorial and administrative contribution.

Douglas Eden
Frederick Short

Contributors

Professor Giuseppe Are	Professor of Contemporary History in the faculty of political science at the University of Pisa. Author of many articles and books on Italian politics.
Luigi Barzini	Liberal Member of the Italian Chamber of Deputies from 1958-72. Author of numerous books including *The Italians*, and a regular contributor to *Encounter* and other periodicals.
Congressman David R. Bowen	Member (Democrat, Mississippi) of the US House of Representatives. A former Harvard Scholar at Oxford University. Member of the House of Representatives Committee on Foreign Affairs.
Douglas Eden	Senior Lecturer in History and Politics at Middlesex Polytechnic, London. Holds two degrees in diplomatic history and is the author of numerous articles on contemporary politics and trade union

affairs. Member (Labour) of the Greater London Council, 1973-77. An originator (1975) and currently Secretary of the Social Democratic Alliance.

Paul Friedrich

Lecturer in Politics at Bonn, West Germany. Formerly a Visiting Fellow at Nuffield College, Oxford. Currently Kennedy Fellow in the Centre for European Studies at Harvard University.

Dr Roy Godson

Associate Professor of Government and Director of the International Labour Programme at Georgetown University, Washington DC. Author of several books on labour and contemporary European political problems including *American Labour and European Politics* and (with Dr Stephen Haseler) *Eurocommunism* (1978).

David Gress

Writer and lecturer on political developments in Scandinavia. Organizer of the recently founded European Institute in Denmark.

Dr Stephen Haseler

Principal Lecturer in Politics at the City of London Polytechnic. Author of several books including *The Gaitskellites* (1969), *The Death of British Democracy* (1976) and *The Tragedy of Labour* (1980). Member (Labour) of the Greater London Council, 1973-77, and Chairman of General Purposes

	Committee. Chairman of the Social Democratic Alliance.
Paul Johnson	Author of *The Offshore Islanders*, *Enemies of Society* and other books. Journalist and lecturer (former editor of *The New Statesman*) contributing regularly to the national press.
Dr Arrigo Levi	Former editor of *La Stampa*. Regular columnist on international affairs for *The Times* and *Newsweek*.
Philip Natas	Lecturer in Politics at the University of Paris. Member of the French Socialist Party.
Professor Hugh Thomas	Chairman of the Directors at the Centre for Policy Studies. Formerly Professor of History and Chairman of the Graduate School of Contemporary European Studies at the University of Reading. Published works include *The Spanish Civil War*, *The Suez Affair*, *John Strachey* and *An Unfinished History of the World*.

CHAPTER ONE

The European Left: An Historical Perspective

HUGH THOMAS

The language of European politics which we choose to employ, 'Left' and 'Right', can be derived from the day in 1789 when the *noblesse* took the seats to the right hand of the President of the French National Assembly, and the Third Estate those on the left hand. That began a phraseology which has enjoyed extraordinary international usage, though it is worth recalling that for over a hundred years, indeed until well after the formation of the Labour party, the usage was uncommon in England: the Left is defined, for example, in the *Complete Oxford Dictionary* (1902) as 'in continental legislatures, the democratic or progressive wing' of the parliamentarians.

'Left' was used colloquially in England about the Labour party before 1914, but only colloquially, and even now the words Right and Left still have just a hint of slang about them. However, parties in Britain do not, as a rule, call themselves Left or Right. They wait to be labelled so by their opponents.

Particularly in politics, words mean a great deal, and here no doubt is a marked difference between Britain and the Continent. Left, Right and Centre have constantly been used on the continental mainland since the mid-nineteenth century as if they meant something explicit, and

France is not the only country where this is applicable. The British verbal *pudeur* in this respect is one more little link between us and the United States, whose parties still happily do not fit into such French revolutionary designations.

Therefore, as I see it, the Left is the conglomeration of political movements which, since about 1860 or so, have in most European states tried to take over the nation's resources in the alleged interest of the whole nation. As such, it is a movement which has wrestled not always successfully with the problem of combining those plans with the preservation of political liberty. Indeed, sometimes, as in Russia and Eastern Europe, it has given up or has never made the effort to preserve liberty, and concentrated on the management of the takeover.

The doubts caused even by the actions of those to whom political liberty is more than a phrase, is such that many observers realise, as do our friends in the USA, that, although there may be a crisis of Western European capitalism, which might be expected (considering the wounds which capitalism has suffered), there is undoubtedly a crisis of socialism.

In all the European countries, including Britain, we see socialist parties grappling unsuccessfully with the problem of how to preserve liberty, yet still longing to introduce characteristic socialist legislation, such as nationalization, in order to achieve control by the state of what Aneurin Bevan called the 'commanding heights of the economy' – a military metaphor picked up from Lenin.

These arguments between Left and Right, semantically though I have tried to dismiss them, have constituted the most serious problem to occur this century in the greater part of Europe. Indeed in most countries of Europe this dilemma has led to civil war or something close to it. This is an important point, for we should not think of Spain, Greece and Russia as being the only states which have experienced brutal civil wars this century: Germany sporadically between 1919 and 1933, Italy in 1920-22 and again in 1943-45, and, in effect, Yugoslavia between 1941-46, and Poland and much of Eastern Europe between 1940-45. Paradoxically, Britain, the only large European country which did not share such an experience, is the country which today appears to possess the sharpest internal problems. Although it is sometimes said that Britain's current problems are due to not being occupied in the Second World War, I should like to put it differently: namely, that the old British structures of society did not collapse between, say, 1933 and 1945, as they did elsewhere, where reconstruction was necessary.

With regard to the present: the difficulties facing the democratic socialists now seem so great at first sight as to justify complacency on the part of their opponents. For example, the British Labour party, once the 'natural party of government', is, in the 1980s, apparently proving that it is incapable of governing. This is not an alluring prospect for a party which established itself as the country's second party of the state in the 1920s.

Then take France, where there has not been a Socialist prime minister for twenty-two years. Only on a few occasions before 1957 have the Socialists dominated a coalition government, and then never for more than Guy Mollet's fourteen months in 1956-57 (in 1936-37, 1946, 1946-47 and 1956-57), not a good prospect for a party which had its first Cabinet minister, Alexandre Millerand, in 1899.

Likewise Spain, where, except during the civil war, with Largo Caballero, the Socialists have never directed a government. The party in Spain even failed in the two free elections of 1977 and 1979 to beat the arbitrarily gathered together collection of ex-Francoists, led by Adolfo Suarez, a man without any experience outside the Franco system.

Similarly Italy, where the Socialist party has never held

office at all, except as a junior member of coalitions led by Christian Democrats.

Germany has a Socialist administration, at least in formal terms, run by a party which is the heir of the movement founded by Lassalle in the 1860s. But it would not be unkind to suggest that its power derives from the fact that, at Bad Godesberg in 1959, it abandoned socialism.

Of course, as David Gress reminds us in his chapter in this book, the socialists have been in power for many years in Sweden and some smaller states, but the pattern of political power in Brussels or Stockholm does not dictate the political character of a continent.

Yet any complacency, always to be distrusted among the opponents of the Left in Europe, would be unwise.

First, every democracy in Europe has within it, powerful, and in some cases large, totalitarian Left parties. Britain is in the peculiar position of having a powerful but tiny Communist party. France has a Communist party which, on occasions since the war, has been the second party in the state, and still is able to veto the formation of a democratic socialist government. In Italy the Communist party has been the second party in the state since 1945. In Spain the Communists are the third party in the state. Considering the record of communist behaviour everywhere when in power, it is remarkable and inexplicable that they should have done so consistently well in so many countries.

In France, Italy and Spain the largest and most efficient trade unions are managed by communists, even if many non-communists are members, and it is common knowledge that the British communists occupy a place in the trade union movement out of all proportion to their numbers in the nation as a whole.

All these communist parties have usually cast a shadow, which differs in size or texture from nation to nation, over the democratic socialist parties. One need only recall the strongly pro-Soviet writings of Labour party thinkers such as the Webbs (in their old age) and Harold Laski, or the conduct of Pietro Nenni and many such socialists in the 1930s, to begin to establish this point.

Though neither socialists nor communists have been able to win many national elections, they have been successful at municipal level, enabling councillors of the Left to control local politics and patronage. This local or regional power base has enabled the Left to pose a challenge to national governments which often have been in better hands.

If it becomes the rule rather than the exception that the main opposition party in the state is to be considered an outlaw by a freedom-loving electorate, then European politics will enter a dangerous, perhaps critical phase. This has effectively been the state of affairs in Italy ever since 1920. Had the Communists won at any stage, who knows what would have happened. The same is now true in France. In 1978 the Socialists and Communists were linked together by the Common Programme, a new version of the Popular Front. The same may be true of Britain in 1984 if the Labour party continues its present road.

Furthermore, a national majority for a certain course of action may be overturned by a minority of well-placed people on the Left who, with determination, intelligence or insolence, will defy this majority; in certain circumstances – a war alert, for example – the situation could turn critical.

We all recall that one of the reasons for the fall of France in 1940 was the loyalty which large sections of the working class felt for Moscow; indeed, in 1940 Maurice Thorez, a deserter, was already in Moscow. As documents recently published from the archives of the southern French prefectures make clear, even in 1950 a Russian offensive (not an impossible eventuality) would have been accompanied by sabotage by communist activists in the heart of France itself. Therefore, it would be an illusion to suppose that this kind of treacherous and subversionary European communism has disappeared in the era of so-called 'Eurocommunism'. The same might apply to Britain, in which trade unions have been organized in sensitive defence support industries.

This brings me to the trade union movement, which need not necessarily and in all circumstances be considered a part of the Left. American experience reminds us of this point, as does that, to some extent, of West Germany. In some countries there are right-wing trade union leaders like Frank Chapple, and there have been many trade union leaders who, like Ernest Bevin or Léon Jouhaux, have been on the 'Right of the Left'. 'Left' and 'Right' in trade union terms do not always mean what they may infer to outsiders. Even so, we are concerned here with a zone of industrial affairs, ranging from approximately 50 per cent of the labour force now in Britain to approximately 20 per cent now in France, where one branch or another of the Left (sometimes democratic, sometimes totalitarian) has established itself, and is accompanied by implicit or explicit syndicalist impulses.

Another difference between Britain and the Continent is that the British Labour movement is now once again the reflection of the interests (insofar as they can be sensibly understood) of the unions, whereas on the Continent the unions tend to reflect the attitudes of one or other of the political parties. This has clearly had an important effect on the texture of English politics in heightening the class struggle in a country where reasons for class hatreds are surely far less valid than they have ever been before.

Whatever may be suggested about the unlikelihood of the Left obtaining power in Europe, it remains a depressing fact that most nominally democratic socialist parties have recently undergone profound changes, and for the worse. Thirty years ago Labour's Foreign Minister, Ernest Bevin, took the lead in constructing the North Atlantic Treaty. In 1956 it was Labour's George Brown, *not* the Conservative prime minister, who challenged Khrushchev over the fate of Eastern European democratic politicians. It was a Socialist administration, led by Paul Ramadier and Jules Moch, who, in late 1947, successfully resolved the most dangerous crisis in post-war France when the Communist party made a determined effort to carry the Cold War onto the streets. But would a present-day French Socialist party be as resolute in a crisis if Communists obtained ministries in a joint administration? It seems unlikely. In the general West European context, the relative virility of German social democracy does not by itself compensate for the declining anti-Sovietism exhibited by the British and French socialist parties; particularly so in a period in which the intellectual inheritance of Bad Godesberg may have almost exhausted itself — and certainly so internationally if Herr Egon Bahr and Herr Herbert Wehner have their way.

This brief *tour d'horizon* of the European Left suggests that there exists throughout the Western end of the European Continent a marked difference between the *pays légal*, reflected in general elections, in which all things considered the Left has done rather badly during the sixty-five years since 1914, and the *pays réel*, where the Left has successfully entrenched itself in many important subsections of the state.

This is a dangerous condition, especially since we have been witnessing a growth in the desire of minorities to defy both law and state by taking law into their own hands. In extreme terms this disaffection takes the form of emergent terrorist groups who cause damage out of all proportion to their numbers, and also of the obdurate (and often illegal) pretensions of left-wing trade unionists.

Policies normally associated with the Left, such as state intervention in the economy, nationalization, centralization, and increasingly the growth of bureaucracy, are not the legacies necessarily or even mainly of left-wing governments. To prove this point we need only to turn to Italy, with its huge state sector, which is a country where Communists and Socialists were in power for but a short time after 1945, as part of de Gasperi's first coalition. No democratic socialist government *anywhere* has undertaken more intervention than Western wartime coalitions during both world wars – facts which were noticed (and regretted) at the time.

The Liberal government in Britain in 1894 ushered in the era of employing fiscal policy for social purposes. Its successor between 1906 and 1914 was the British administration which, in the words of Elie Halévy, succeeded in 'transforming the old England of individualism and laissez faire into an England organized from above'. Bismarck inspired much of Europe's social insurance, and state intervention or management of industry had been the rule in many economies before 1900, though not in Britain. France, not the best-loved hero of the Left, was a prime mover in Spanish social reform and nationalization. To most judicious minds the general phenomenon loosely known as Fascism (including Nazism) was much more a 'heresy of the Left' (as the Spanish Communist Joaquín Maurín put it) than an 'extreme' version of conservatism. National Socialism certainly had a closer family relationship with the Left than it had with the orthodox Right.

Finally, no survey of the general position of the European Left in the twentieth century can avoid the point that the Europe of which we usually talk is only half of this small continent. In the other Eastern half, a totalitarian Left is in power. If the Iron Curtain should ever be removed we shall all see to what degree those countries of the East, including what used to be European Russia, share our traditions. Nothing that has happened since 1945 has really dimmed that sense of European identity. A historic Europe cannot exclude Prague, Budapest, Cracow, or even Königsberg, the birthplace of Kant, now mysteriously concealed under the bogus name of Kaliningrad.

Four concluding points are necessary in any general survey of the history of the European Left. The first, previously mentioned, concerns the gap between the British and the continental experience. There is no doubt that the long history of the evolution of British constitutional arrangements (complete before the Left was even conceived of in politics) gave to British socialism a constitutional bias at the beginning. Marx may have written as a guest of England and drawn most of his examples from English experience, but the kind of revolution which he thought likely was more improbable in England than anywhere else. That rigorous search for a philosophical basis to socialism, his desire for a theory of politics which would establish laws for society as rigid as those of science, and his craving for a lay religion which characterized much continental socialism, was foreign to the old English way of doing things.

Only in the late 1960s and the 1970s has there been a return to such yearnings. Was this perhaps the real meaning of Britain's new understanding with the countries of the European community? The tribute which English virtue suddenly felt a need to pay to continental vices? So it seemed for a time as students of the English New Left puzzled their way through the byways of Gramsci and learned new words like 'hegemony'. But the new brutalism of the English Left, amply displayed by the vulgar syndicalism of the winter of 1978-79, cannot surely be blamed on Europe. After all, continental grave-diggers may have sometimes resented burying the bodies of the bourgeoisie, but I am not sure that they ever said so.

This new phase of brutalism is, I fear, something specifically English – new English, not old English – deriving from a country where class consciousness has been successfully, negatively, destructively heightened in the last generation. Its crescendo in the winter of 1979 was accompanied by moments when it seemed that the Labour government had handed over power to strike committees. However, this may be seen as a turning point in our political history, one which secured for the conservatism of Mrs Thatcher that formidable majority in the May general election.

The second point is a very general one which affects all countries of Europe and even every variety of left-wing experience. The Left has two distinct roots, both of which derive from pre-industrial sources. There are the age-old social protests of workers or slaves which are as ancient as civilization itself; and there has been the equally age-old dream of intellectuals to create a society of equals, a perfectly planned society or a 'New Jerusalem' couched in the days of the Renaissance as a 'priesthood of all believers' and from the eighteenth century onwards in rational, lay or violently anticlerical terms. The history of the Left has been in every country the history of the tension between those two basically irreconcilable aims.

Irreconcilable because when it comes to the point, the vast majority of workers (the Spanish anarchists being an exception) have not aspired to live in an ideal, rational or even an atheistic republic. They have wanted to be rich and prosperous, to be able to feed their families adequately, and to be free. I am afraid that intellectuals on the Left have never quite appreciated this point. They have thought, as Albert Sorel said of the *philosophes* in the eighteenth century, that once they were in power 'not only the face of the world, but the very soul of man would be changed'. This, of course is an illusion, though a strong one.

Thirdly, the Left has lived with an even greater and more romantic illusion, the notion that the industrial working class have something in common with a 'chosen race'. This was, I think, Marx's most enduring contribution to human illusion, one which will probably outlive his claim to have invented ideal laws of society comparable to those of science, or the invention of his own extraordinary heavy vocabulary, full of 'social scum' and 'lackeys', or his highly undesirable arousal of long-term hopes of an abolition of the state in order to justify the dictatorship of the proletariat for the transitional stage to communism.

Yet, surely the nineteenth-century immigrants into the jerry-built cities of Lille, Manchester, Essen and Barcelona had every reason to believe themselves a 'chosen people', the cannon fodder of capitalism? Unfortunately, as Raymond Aron has pointed out in a number of fine books, there was never really very much in common between the men of Lille and the men of Manchester. They were separated by distinct national loyalties rather than united by 'class', and nationalism was always stronger than international solidarity. Indeed, the whole concept of an 'elect' industrial working class seemed most unjust to, say, shop workers, who (at least in the nineteenth century) worked longer hours than anyone else, domestic servants (the largest professional group in London in 1900), and even agricultural workers, artists and intellectuals. Yet the myth survived and even now survives in a few rarified senior common rooms, though not in working men's clubs.

Fourthly, we cannot ignore even in a rudimentary survey, the sinister, perhaps disastrous, relationship between many on the European Left and Russia following the October revolution of 1917. We have witnessed in the West what one observer of the Labour movement has described as a 'Russia complex'.

Briefly, we must realize that the Russians are a

European people whose form of government has never shaken off the unfortunate experience of Tartar rule in the Middle Ages, a rule which accustomed people to believe that they could expect of government nothing but butchery, taxation and injustice. The Russians, partly in consequence, never experienced feudalism in the Western European sense, nor capitalism, and therefore at the time of Marx were living disproof of his theories: the nobles were civil servants; the manufacturers were, as a rule, either foreigners acting on a licence from the government or were actually working for the government. Unlike the history of most countries, Russia's history under the Tsars became more and more repressive. Richard Pipes described Alexander III's legislation of the 1880s as having the same connection with totalitarianism as Magna Carta has with liberty.

Nevertheless, for reasons which we all know, Russia, for much of the twentieth century, has been seen either as a future which was working or as the focus for extraordinary loyalties and abject disciplines throughout Europe.

The inter-relation between these fantasies and the history of the working class in Europe has given a final element of absurdity to our contemporary history, which would seem richly comic if it were not so often accompanied by treachery, murder and self-deception on a Homeric scale.

The politics of the Western European Left may seem a troublesome terrain, but one which does not yet threaten to alter the Western landscape. America may feel secure. As Keynes once said of England, 'England still stands outside Europe: Europe's voiceless tremors do not reach her', so some might today say of the USA. Certainly the American experience has avoided mass socialism. For reasons explored by Werner Sombart seventy years ago, the USA has not developed a mass socialist movement. Also, although America has quantities of its great cities dominated by particular groups of immigrants, it has never had whole areas of its nation dominated by what Annie Kriegel, in her brilliant book, *The French Communists* (Chicago, 1972), called a 'counter community': a section of the country already essentially a dependency of the Soviet Union before any conquest, with some industries – such as the railways – and some towns dominated by Communists for two generations.

Yet even though the USA does not have a heavily politicized labour force nor an effective socialist party, state intervention in industry remains a significant problem which the USA shares with Europe. More ominously, America shows signs of a loss of will, greater now perhaps than that displayed elsewhere in the West. Some of the politicians in the Democratic party seem as if they have been to a Fabian summer school addressed by Francois Mitterrand and chaired by Herr Egon Bahr. Just when some European politicians are beginning to persuade us, successfully, at long last, of the banal, long-neglected truth that prosperity is likely to derive above all from a revival of free enterprise, the United States seems to be beginning to impose upon her free enterprise mortal wounds.

This loss of will internally is reflected in an international diplomacy apparently bent on insisting that the Cold War has passed its meridian. This is at the time when Russian threats to Europe have never been greater and when Russian actions, directly or indirectly, in Central America, the Caribbean, Southern Africa, the Middle East and Central Asia have been as insistent as they have been impudent. Such activities must raise the question as to whether even 'Cold War' is any longer an adequate term for what is in reality a very dangerous confrontation.

In such circumstances any real or prolonged weakness of

will on the part of the leaders of the US far outweighs in
importance for the European future any number of
proclamations from European drawing-room socialists,
Bollinger Bolsheviks or whisky Trotskyists. Although the
internal politics of the various Western European nations,
and trends within the Left in those nations, are of great
significance, this collection of essays must be seen in the
context of *general* Western geopolitical defensiveness.

CHAPTER TWO

British Labour and the West

STEPHEN HASELER

A Contemporary Historical Perspective

Since the Second World War the British Labour party and movement has taken part in a broad bipartisan approach to British foreign policy. Although there have been divergences between the major political parties, the most dramatic and serious being the disagreement over the Suez affair in 1956, neither Labour nor the Conservatives have wavered from a resolute commitment to the Western alliance system.

Indeed, it was the post-war Labour administration led by Clement Attlee, with Ernest Bevin as Foreign Secretary, that took the lead amongst the nations of Europe in establishing the North Atlantic Treaty Organization. This same administration gave full diplomatic and military support to the United States in the United Nations action in Korea in the late 1940s and early 1950s. However, in so doing it incurred an unprecedentedly high peace-time defence budget that was arguably unsustainable, and was later cut back by the 1951 Churchill administration.

When Labour went into opposition in 1951, a period out of office which was to last for thirteen years, Labour's social democratic leadership under Attlee, and later under his successor, Gaitskell, continued this bipartisan policy. Labour's leadership withstood challenges from the Left of the party on a whole range of issues that had implications for Britain's pro-alliance strategic posture. For example, Labour supported German rearmament in 1954; it stood by the Conservatives when they decided to maintain Britain's independent nuclear deterrent and it continued to support US nuclear bases on British soil and in British waters. In the early 1960s Labour's leadership came under severe pressure from some of its activists to unilaterally abandon Britain's nuclear deterrent and to call for the withdrawal of US Polaris bases in Scotland, but it withstood these pressures.

When Labour returned to government in 1964 the traditional bipartisanship was reasserted. Labour did withdraw from 'East of Suez' but its central NATO commitment and consequent obligations remained inviolate. During Labour's period in government after 1974 it secured Britain's membership of the European Community, a central strategic aim of its main NATO partners, particularly the Low Countries, the Federal Republic and the United States. Labour was bitterly divided over the Common Market issue and this division did not break down on classical Left versus Right lines. Even so, and irrespective of the merits of the case for or against entry, the Labour administrations under both Wilson and Callaghan ensured that Britain remained firmly wedded to the Western political, defence and trading systems.

Furthermore, a powerful case can be made out, and often is by informed commentators, that in the thirty years since the inception of NATO, Labour administrations have been rather more 'Atlanticist' in their inclinations than have Conservative governments. This was a point often made about the Callaghan government (1976-79).

The point of this short excursion into the foreign policy of Labour in the past three decades is to set in context the fundamental nature of the transformation that Labour may now be about to undergo in terms of its general attitudes to the alliance, to the Western trading system and to the East-West issue.

An Emerging Neutralism?

Throughout Labour's history there has been present in the party a small, contained, but influential body of opinion that has sought after what it has described as 'a socialist foreign policy'. The nature of such 'a socialist foreign policy' has never been properly articulated and to this day remains inchoate. Broadly speaking this minority tradition has been critical of Labour's foreign policy establishment on two counts. First, it has objected to the level of defence expenditure incurred by successive post-war administrations and particularly to the portion of it devoted to nuclear weapons. This critique of British defence policy draws upon an eclectic Left tradition within the Labour movement, upon pacifism, nuclear pacifism, utopianism, Christian, particularly Methodist, socialism, as well as the more hard-line Marxist, fellow-travelling and pro-Soviet tradition. The arguments most typically used to advance this critique of the level of defence spending are both moral and economic, for the belief of traditional pacificism gains added credence when viewed alongside the present level of defence spending, which the British economy cannot support if it is to maintain its welfare objectives.

Secondly, there has been a long-standing criticism within the Labour party of what the Left has termed Labour's pro-American or 'Cold War' posture. The belief is deeply embedded on the Labour Left that a socialist foreign policy should be rather more neutral than it has been as between what is often described as capitalist America and socialist or communist Russia. This has led some sections of the Labour Left into developing third force ideas about Britain's role in the world. These third force notions have taken various forms over the years, from opposition to Britain's membership of NATO, to the advocacy of a united but neutral democratic socialist Europe, to rather fanciful conceptions of Britain assuming the leadership of a Third World bloc.

Needless to suggest, these critiques have not yet been translated by the Labour Left into a coherent alternative global political strategy which can be effectively counterpoised to that of the pro-Western Labour establishment.

However, it is a central thesis of this short chapter that as the Labour party apparatus, as opposed to the parliamentary leadership, moved to the Left during the 1970s, Labour's commitment to the West was commensurately weakened to the point where an emergent neutralism is now perceivable. This emerging neutralism can be seen on two levels. First, on the level of party foreign and defence policy documents, and secondly, on the level of Labour's changed attitude to party-to-party relations with East bloc regimes.

A particularly instructive method of gauging Labour's changing world-view is to look at *Labour's Programme, 1976*, the policy document for the medium-term future agreed by the Labour party at its annual conference of that year. Such policy documents are a sensible guide to underlying trends within the party, certainly more so than party manifestos which are inevitably tailored for immediate electoral purposes. Furthermore *Labour's Programme, 1976* is a relatively settled statement of position, more enduring and less transient than individual speeches or statements. This document was also the first product of the long-term thinking of Labour's newly Left-dominated National Executive Committee. The Left gained overall control of the party executive in 1973 and so this statement represents about three years' considered work.

I propose to outline the main points of argument of the document and introduce where appropriate previous Labour party statements in order to stress the new and radical direction ushered in by the left-wing executive.

The 1976 policy, which remains Labour's policy today, makes no specific commitment to NATO. By contrast, Labour's policy in 1960 was set out forcefully: 'We must accept the obligations we have undertaken and remain loyal supporters of NATO, in the creation of which . . . the Labour government played a leading role'.[1] The nearest that the 1976 statement comes to affirming support for NATO is when it argues: 'Labour recognizes that it has a responsibility to work for *these policies* particularly within the EEC and NATO' (my italics).

Yet *these policies*, which are outlined in a whole page of the document, represent a total break with Labour's tradition both in tone and substance. For instance, Labour's executive argues that Britain's foreign policy goals can be achieved 'only in alliance with socialist and liberation movements abroad'. Yet these movements are not defined. Also, the document has invocations against 'the exploitative nature of British capitalism' and other such loose, quasi-Marxist phraseology, and it is in the context of the language of liberation and socialism that the foreign policy for Labour is set.

Indeed the 1976 document tilts the whole axis of Labour's foreign policy in a new direction. It is suffused with such rhetoric as 'breaking down the bloc mentality'; it states that 'the Labour Party is committed to the ultimate mutual and concurrent dissolution of NATO and the Warsaw Pact', a proposition that has never been accepted as NATO policy. The document further argues that: 'We have yet to see any progress towards the removal of the American nuclear bases . . . We believe that it should now be possible to achieve the agreed withdrawal of these bases'.

On Britain's defence contribution the Labour executive argues for 'Cuts . . . of £1,000 million a year by 1980'. It argues that in order to achieve such reductions some mix of the following options should be undertaken: a rundown of Britain's Polaris force and facilities, the elimination of all costs to Britain of army combat forces outside Europe, a smaller ship fleet, reduced British ground-force levels in Europe, a lower cost air force, and reductions in associated support programmes.

The 1976 document makes no mention of the threat posed to Britain's or the West's security by the Soviet Union and its armaments build-up. A whole section of the policy statement is devoted to a 'rejection of US interventionism', particularly in Latin America, but there is no attempt to balance this condemnation by a similar denunciation of the Soviet Union in Eastern Europe.

This 1976 statement by Labour's executive was little noticed at the time of publication because Britain then had a Labour administration which refused to translate it and its tone into national policy. Yet it now assumes great importance as Labour enters into an opposition period in which the executive's authority is enhanced vis-à-vis that of the parliamentary leadership. It is an early sign of an emergent neutralism.

Since 1976 the Labour party has further developed its alternative strategy for dealing with Britain's domestic problems. This alternative strategy has important implications for Britain's relations with its Western allies and its general role in the world. It had its genesis in the Tribune group of the Left Labour MPs but now also has the support of Britain's federation of trade unions, the TUC, and a large section of the Labour party. The strategy involves proposals for a wide range of import controls, for compulsory planning agreements between leading firms and the state, and for the nationalization of British banks and insurance companies. Labour, at its conference in 1979, passed a motion calling for British withdrawal from the European Economic Community if Labour's demands for changes in financing were not accepted.

Labour's alternative strategy, protectionist and socialist at home and incipiently neutralist abroad, is not yet accepted by Labour's parliamentary leadership. Yet its central assumptions have powerful support from sections of intellectual opinion in Britain, particularly the Cambridge economists. Also, its potential for securing popular backing, especially in a national economic crisis, should not be wholly discounted.

Concurrently with these changes in policy Labour's executive has embarked upon a radical new direction in its party-to-party relations with East bloc regimes. Labour remains a member of the Socialist International, the international organization of democratic socialist and social democratic political parties. Labour's traditional policy was to restrict its international contacts to member parties such as the West German SPD and the Israeli Labour party. The party used to refuse overtures from East bloc regimes, but this policy has now been reversed. Labour's executive, starting in 1973, has entered into fraternal relations with a host of communist regimes. Labour party officials have travelled as representatives to most of the East bloc parties including the CPSU, and the executive now regularly invites observers from these parties to its annual conferences. The rationale used by the executive for these unprecedented party-to-party contacts remains Labour's support for détente. Critics of these new contacts such as the former Prime Minister Callaghan point to the generally accepted thesis that détente entails an improvement in relations between states and peoples, not parties. Indeed, Callaghan has publicly stated that détente does not mean the abandonment of the ideological struggle between East and West and that such party-to-party contacts only serve to give legitimacy to the regimes of the East bloc.

Labour's executive has also established relations with some of the Eurocommunist parties of Southern Europe, particularly with the PCI, PCF and PCE (Italian, French and Spanish communist parties).

Ben Pimlott, a Labour historian, has suggested that 'the British Labour Party is now the most socialist of the European social democratic parties'. This depiction is not exaggerated. However, a detailed study of Labour's recent policy pronouncements, including those outside the foreign policy area, display a sweep and intent that is radically different from social democracy as it has been understood in Western Europe since the war. There are two fundamental respects in which the present Labour party organization can fairly be characterized as departing from the social democratic tradition. First, Labour no longer formally commits itself to the mixed economy as a desirable goal but now argues for a fundamental transformation of society to socialism which is invariably associated with wholesale common ownership. As part of its retreat from social democracy Labour has recently introduced into Britain's political vocabulary a fascinating new notion, the concept of irreversibility. In *Labour's Programme, 1976* the party declares itself as being in favour of 'an irreversible shift in the balance of power and wealth in favour of working people and their families'. There is no definition offered of 'working people' but the irreversible concept is a glimpse into the political mentality and general theoretical framework also encountered in the work of Eurocommunist theoreticians.

As a measure of the change that has overtaken Labour this kind of approach should be contrasted with the statement in the 1960 party policy, that 'both public and private enterprise have a place in the economy'. No similar statement appears in the 1976 document.

Secondly, throughout recent Labour party policy pronouncements there is a distinct anti-Americanism. As with many of the Eurocommunist parties, specific policy recommendations are of less interest than the underlying sentiments. The United States is typically referred to as 'imperialist' whereas this term is not applied to the Soviet Union. The United States is described as 'aggressive' or 'potentially aggressive' whereas the Soviet Union is viewed as defensive. Hence the belief in lower Western defence expenditures. However, post-Vietnam US introspection and seemingly lower resolve in world affairs appears not to affect this assessment of US motives by the Labour Left.

Intriguingly, the British Labour party's executive tends to side with the Soviet Union in the Sino-Soviet dispute.[2] This broadly is also the stance of the major communist parties of Southern Europe. Labour's Left leaders are continually warning about 'playing the China card'.

Power in the Labour Party and the Future

By 1980 the majority of the Parliamentary Labour Party (PLP) and Labour's leadership had managed to resist this emergent neutralism which characterizes the Labour party apparatus. Although both the Labour party and the TUC have embraced the alternative strategy, the Parliamentary Labour Party has not. In fact, the PLP remains for the moment the last bastion of social democracy within the British Labour movement. For this reason the present controversy within the party about the power of the PLP and its leader assumes momentous importance. Therefore, the whole future direction of the British Labour party may rest upon the outcome of the present seemingly arcane constitutional wrangles.

At the Labour party conference at Brighton in October 1979 the Labour Left attempted to secure three constitutional changes which would have the effect of reducing the independence of the PLP by making it more answerable to the party apparatus and hence to its dominant left wing. The Left achieved victory on two of their three constitutional proposals: they failed in an attempt to reconstruct the mechanism for selecting the party leader but they succeeded both in giving virtual complete control to the party executive in drawing up the manifesto at election times and in securing mandatory reselection by local Labour party caucuses of their Labour Members of Parliament.

By far the most significant issue is the mandatory reselection procedure for Labour MPs. As in most of the industrial democracies, party activists at local level are more radical and ideological than their representatives in the legislature, but in Labour's case the situation at local level is alarming. Labour party membership has declined dramatically in recent years, particularly in inner-city areas where most Labour MPs are located. There has also been a marked social change in local membership. This essentially amounts to a flight away from Labour of the affluent skilled working class which has traditionally been the backbone of its activist support. In the vast majority of Labour-held constituencies the local caucuses are now dominated by small groups of middle-class quasi-professional, public sector employees, many of the Trotskyite by inclination and rhetoric, and hostile to the moderates and social democrats in the PLP.

As power passes to these local caucuses so moderate Labour MPs come under increasing pressure to conform to the policies and attitudes of the Left-dominated party executive. If moderate MPs attempt to withstand this pressure, under the new rules they can be 'de-selected' as candidates as a matter of routine. During the last

Parliament a number of moderate MPs were in fact de-selected. In this Parliament, as the mechanism of de-selection becomes embedded and institutionalized, the number will be much greater. Labour MPs who fall foul of their local organizations are unable to appeal to the ordinary voters because Britain possesses no primary system.

Labour's social democratic leadership can respond to this serious challenge from the Left in one of two ways. It can continue to work within the framework of the party and accept the constitutional changes. This will inevitably result in the emergence of a PLP that accepts or is forced to accept the broad socialist position of Labour's executive. Such a transformation of the PLP could even take place during the lifetime of this Parliament, so that when the next general election takes place ALL the organs of the Labour party will be under effective Left control.

Alternatively Labour's parliamentary leadership could decide to fight the constitutional changes, declare that it will not accept them and create within the Labour movement two rival centres of power. Harold Wilson, drawing upon the analogy of Rome and Avignon, recently suggested that Labour's present disputes could lead to the emergence of two Popes. If this kind of schismatic tendency develops then an organic split within the Labour party cannot be ruled out. The creation of a new left-of-centre party shorn of its Marxist component might be attractive to wide sections of the public.

Britain's future relationship with the Western political, defence and trading systems may indeed turn upon how effectively the Labour Left can be either contained or isolated. Even if the Labour Left, advancing its alternative strategy, should succeed in capturing all the organs of the party and avoiding a split, it should be understood that Labour's electoral strength is on a declining curve. At the recent general election, Labour received a lower percentage of the popular vote than in the election of 1935 which was generally considered to be a near disaster for the party. In the last three general elections Labour has not climbed above the 40 per cent barrier,[3] and its active membership has fallen dramatically over the last decade. Its individual, voluntary membership is so low that Labour can hardly claim any longer to be a mass party.[4]

It is conceivable that should Labour's social democratic leadership in Parliament either be ousted or decide to conform to the politics of the Left executive, then Labour's electoral decline will become even more pronounced. Much will depend upon how the Conservatives and Liberals exploit the developing situation.

Even with Labour's continuing weakness at electoral level there are other factors which could decisively affect Britain's medium-term political future. In terms of general economic and political power Britain's trade unions play a major role, more so than in any other Western industrialized nation. British union elites will continue to act as a powerful interest group which will ineluctably remain a force exerting pressure on government for increased protectionism, increased public spending, and arguably increased inflation by forcing governments to print money. In a future situation of high unemployment, trade union elites and some members may become increasingly attracted to alternative strategies, siege economies and the like as a way out of the economic malaise. The fact that this route would lead to greater impoverishment may not matter; the emotional and psychological attraction of an alternative solution will count for much more than the intellectually constructed arguments against it.

With a scenario of high unemployment, social dislocation and political polarization, the political predilections of Britain's trade union elites will be crucial.

Social democrats and 'Labourists'[5] are still present at the top tables of the TUC, especially in the Electricians' and Engineering Unions. However, the political complexion of the central leadership of the TUC has changed radically since the early 1960s. Britain's largest union, the Transport and General Workers, and many of the rapidly expanding white-collar public sector unions, now have elites whose political traditions make them much more amenable to calls for a socialist transformation of society and an alternative strategy. In short, in any future industrial or political confrontation many of Britain's most powerful trade union leaders will view the crisis as a political opportunity to transform the fundamental nature of British society.

The vast majority of Britain's workforce will not see things in the same political terms. The workforce and their families continue to perceive strikes and industrial militancy in terms solely of securing improved wages and conditions; the political dimension is virtually absent. Britain's future, including the nation's relations with the West, may well rest in part upon how effectively the POLITICAL attitudes of Britain's workforce, which remain broadly social democratic, are represented by trade union and Labour party elites.

Britain's economic problems and industrial dislocation have not as yet radicalized Britain's workforce, as the results of the 1979 general election amply display. It is this radicalization, the growth and grip of various shades of Marxist and pseudo-Marxist ideology, of Britain's trade union elites and intelligentsia that remains the problem.

Notes

1 *From The Amplification of Aims*, passed by the Labour party conference, 1960, at the insistence of the leader of the party, Hugh Gaitskell.

2   In May 1978 Britain's Chief of the Defence Staff visited China and made public comments about Britain and China both having 'an enemy at the door whose capital is Moscow'. Senior members of Labour's executive publicly rebuked Sir Neil Cameron (CODS) for these remarks and some of them called for his resignation. There are numerous other examples of Labour Left thinking regarding the Sino-Soviet dispute.

3   *Election statistics*

1951	48.8%
1974 (February)	37.2%
1974 (October)	39.2%
1979	36.9%

Labour's vote as a percentage of the total electorate:

1951	39.9%
1974 (February)	29.2%
1974 (October)	28.5%
1979	28.1%

4   *Labour party membership*
It is notoriously difficult to be precise about Labour party membership strength. There are two types of member: trade union member and individual member. The individual member is the category that counts because it is here that an individual makes a commitment to the party by voluntarily paying a subscription. All authorities agree that Labour's individual membership has declined dramatically in the last decade; my own estimate is that in reality Labour's membership is much lower than 300,000. However, this membership is by no means a true reflection of the number of active supporters, which is considerably less than 100,000. Therefore Labour can in no sense claim to be a mass party as Britain's population is well over fifty million.

5   'Labourist' is a term widely used to describe the ideology of more traditional Labour leaders and supporters. These are people who essentially see the Labour movement and Labour party in interest terms, as attempting to seek

advance for working people within the system, rather than in ideological terms. 'Labourists' are usually located on the Right of the party. They are often not only non-socialist but anti-socialist. To use an inexact parallel from American political language, 'Labourists' are social conservatives who support a left-of-centre party primarily on economic grounds.

CHAPTER THREE

The British Left, Trade Unions and Democracy

PAUL JOHNSON

There is in Britain a vague and undefined feeling among many people that the Labour movement − that is the Labour party and the trade unions affiliated to the TUC − is in danger of drifting into the hands of the totalitarian Left. How justified is this feeling? How exactly could the totalitarian Left destroy democracy in Britain? And what steps should we take to avert such a threat? I propose to take these three questions in turn.

First, the danger to the Labour party. The Left is now engaged in a full-scale campaign to achieve what they call the 'democratization' of the Labour party. They believe that Labour will be in opposition for the next four to five years and their aim is to complete this programme before Labour takes office again. What do they mean by democratization? They do not mean parliamentary democracy − that is, rule by MPs elected by the entire electorate as trustees of their interest. They mean something quite different. As one of their leaders put it: 'We believe in the Democracy of the Committed.' By 'the Committed' he means the party activists, the militants, those who believe that politics is the most important thing in life and who are prepared to devote themselves, body and soul, to the pursuit of *political* aims. What he means, in short, is oligarchic democracy, if that is not a contradiction in terms, in which a self-constituted and self-perpetuating elite act in what they conceive to be the interests of the masses. Lenin called it 'democratic centralism'. Certain Afro-Asian dictators have another name for it: 'guided democracy'.

How is the 'Democracy of the Committed' to be achieved? In June, the Left published an eight-point programme for the 'democratization' of Labour party decision-making. This argues as follows. First, the party meeting is to become the main forum of debate and the final authority on policy, within the framework of the decisions of the Labour party conference. Second, the party meeting would have the right to discuss all shadow Cabinet recommendations on parliamentary business or proposed appointments. Third, all the principal front bench spokesmen would be elected by open ballot and the distribution of shadow portfolios would be subject to the approval of the party meeting. Four, backbench committees to take over many of the powers of the leadership. Five, regular meetings between the shadow Cabinet and the National Executive to discuss and determine policy and strategy. Six, all Labour staff at Westminster to be controlled and paid by party headquarters, the public funds available for this purpose being diverted to Transport House. Seven, no more Labour party peerages, thus ending one of the party leader's chief sources of patronage. Lastly, and most important, all these arrangements to continue when Labour holds office, thus subjecting the powers of a Labour prime minister and Cabinet to control and veto by the party machine.

These proposals should be taken in conjunction with four other so-called 'reforms'. The first is the appointment and composition of a committee to inquire into the party structure. The second is the proposal that the leader should be elected not by Labour Members of Parliament alone, as happens at present, but by an electoral college, in which the party militants would play an important part. The third is the proposal that the party leader should no longer have a veto over the election manifesto which is drawn up by the National Executive. And the fourth is that all parliamentary candidates, including sitting Members of Parliament, must submit themselves for reselection.

It is perfectly obvious what these proposals are designed to secure. They are designed to bring about a massive shift of power from the parliamentary leadership to the party militants. It is true that some of the proposals, at first glance, would seem to increase the power of backbench MPs vis-à-vis the leader. But this is an illusion. Taken as a whole, the proposals must diminish the freedom of the individual MP. Not only does the need to go through the process of reselection at regular intervals place the MP firmly in the hands of his local management committee (the party caucus), but the fact that his vote at party meetings will be open and published allows that same committee to give him his instructions and monitor his compliance with them. Thus he is turned from a trustee into a mandated delegate. The net effect of the changes, then, is twofold: first, to place the MP firmly in the hands of his local executive; second, to place party policy firmly in the hands of the National Executive.

How far has the Left made progress in getting these proposals adopted? Of the three which were put to the party conference this year, the Left lost in their bid to secure the election of the party leader by an electoral college. This is actually one of the least important of their objectives and, as the other changes take effect, it is certain to be carried in due course. On the other two issues — control of the election manifesto and the reselection of MPs — the latter by far the most important of all, they won without difficulty. They have also won a very important battle over the composition of the Committee of Inquiry into the party, from which they have succeeded in excluding any representation by Labour MPs and on which the Left is now certain to have a decisive majority.

It may be asked, why this animus against Labour MPs? What does it signify? The desire to diminish the power of MPs and to subject what remains of it to party control is motivated by one simple consideration: the MP is the one type of party official the militants cannot elect or appoint. In the last resort the MP is elected or dismissed by the voters as a whole, in the privacy of the ballot box.

But, one may further ask, is not the National Executive of the Labour party itself an elective body? Does it not represent large numbers of people? The National Executive is a very curious body indeed. Some of its members sit there *ex officio*. Its trade union members, and its women's section, are appointed by a very small number of senior trade union officials. Its constituency members are, it is true, voted for by constituency delegates. They appear to get anything up to 650,000 votes each when the result of the elections is read out to conference. But here we come to a riddle. When is a vote not a vote? And the answer is: when it's a vote for an internal Labour party election. For that figure of 650,000 does not mean that there are 650,000 members of the Labour party. That figure is notional. A constituency party claims to have X number of members. That claim is upheld provided there are X number of subscriptions. The real number is impossible to discover. Nobody knows exactly how many members of the Labour party there are. All that is known is that the figure has been falling for a large number of years. It may be that there are less than 100,000 altogether. I would suggest considerably less. Nor do these members necessarily turn up when the conference delegates are mandated by the local committees. Under Labour party procedure, no attempt is made to ballot individual members by post. They have to appear in person, and most of them choose not to do so. It is my belief that the average constituency Labour party of today is run by no more than a score of active members. Labour is no longer a mass party. It is a party of militant elites. That is why the use of the so-called 'bedsitter vote' has proved so useful in helping the Left to take over so many Labour constituency parties. That is why the use of what are called 'flying delegates' has been so effective in challenging, and in some cases ejecting, sitting Labour MPs who are singled out by the militants for their centrist or right-wing views.

These tactics have been successfully used time and time again, especially in the big cities. If Labour were a mass party, they would not work. If Labour were the party it was in the 1950s – or even up to the mid-1960s – they would not work. They work today because there has been a catastrophic decline – a decline which is grossly underestimated in the official figures – in the number of people prepared to take an active part in Labour party affairs. It is my belief that the actual number of Labour party militants in the whole of Britain is between 10,000 and 20,000. For the purposes of comparison, I should say that my own constituency Conservative party – admittedly one of the biggest in the country – has over 10,000 paid-up members.

What of trade union affiliation to the Labour party? Both in the trade union section and in the women's section of the National Executive, members are supposedly elected by enormous numbers of votes. But these numbers are notional. They do not consist of real people. How many affiliated memberships the individual union takes up is a matter for the union executive to decide and depends on how many membership fees they are prepared to contribute. The system, which is quite indefensible by any standards of democratic representation, rests upon the assumption, which may well have been broadly true when the Labour party was founded in 1900, that a man who wants to join a trade union is likely to want to be a member of the Labour party. But of course, in 1979, we know this to be quite fallacious. At the last election not much more than half of trade union members voted for Labour candidates. Only a tiny fraction of trade unionists attend Labour party meetings.

There is another factor. A large and increasing percentage of trade union members do not join unions because they want to, but because they have no choice in the matter. Under the closed shop system, which is now spreading very rapidly, joining the specified union is a condition of employment. Indeed, in a large number of firms, the employer deducts the union subscription from the employee's pay check, along with income tax and social security contributions. The firm acts as collector for the union. If the worker objects to the money being deducted, as he is legally entitled to do, the employer may dismiss him where a closed shop agreement is in force, without compensation or legal redress. This procedure is made possible under a schedule of the 1974 Trade Union Act. Indeed, failure to join the designated union is about the only reason, under the Employment Protection Act of 1975, which entitles an employer to use dismissal without redress. Of course, even under the closed shop, a worker can decline to pay the part of his union subscription designated as the 'political levy', which goes automatically to the Labour party and is the theoretical justification for the huge number of votes flourished by the union bosses at Labour party conferences. The worker does not have to pay this 'levy', but in declining to do so, he must take the positive action of 'contracting out'. Nor can he merely signify his intention to 'contract out' to the *employer*. The process must be done through the *union* and in most closed shop firms (and in many others too) the employer will continue to deduct the political levy from his wages until officially notified by the union. It is not hard to see that a man requires courage and determination to go through this complicated process. Most do not bother, particularly since they know that a man who insists on 'contracting out' is noted by union officials as a 'trouble maker'. And in a closed shop firm, a man whom union officials classify as a troublemaker is liable to be regarded as one by the management as well.

We should also bear in mind how easy it is for the union machine to expel a 'trouble maker'. Most union rule books contain a rule, or rules, which confer on the appropriate union boss a general or blanket power of expulsion. One big union, for instance, may expel a member for 'conduct whether in connection with (the union), the trade, or otherwise, which is, in the opinion of the Committee, directly or indirectly detrimental to the interests, welfare or reputation of the union'. This is the exact equivalent of the old Section Nine of Queen's Regulations − 'conduct prejudicial to good order and military discipline' − which allowed the army to 'get' a soldier otherwise guiltless of any specific offence.

What this means in practice is that union officials can expel anyone they want to expel. It is a perfect example of absolute power. A research worker who examined the rule books of eighty unions, representing ninety four per cent of the TUC's general membership, found that sixty-six out of eighty rule books contained a clause of this type. In some rule books, deliberate attempts are made to avoid the necessity of spelling out the offence in even the most general terms. In the case of the National Union of Journalists, my union, rule 18 (a) could be used to impose a censorship of the press.

How fiercely are these rules actually enforced? Unions ought at least to observe the principles of natural justice − that is, to serve a notice setting out the charge and making it specific, to hold a proper hearing, to give the accused a chance to defend himself and to confine the hearing to the charge specified. But how can such rules of natural justice be enforced in practice, especially nowadays when loss of union membership usually deprives a man of his livelihood? In fact some rule books specifically repudiate the rules of natural justice. In the case of one big union, the rule book allows the executive to refuse to give the victim any reasons for expelling him and it does not provide either for a notice of the charges or the right to a hearing. Although statute law confers on unions quite extraordinary legal privileges and immunities, it does not require their internal disciplinary system to observe any of the laws of natural justice.

But it may be argued that a trade union is itself a democratic body. In theory, and in some respects, this is an accurate depiction. But it is very characteristic of most British trade unions that little or no attempt is made to secure a high turnout at union elections. Press coverage which arouses the interests of members and encourages a higher vote is almost invariably resented as 'gross interference in the internal affairs of the union'. Some unions forbid candidates to campaign openly. Others fiercely resist the introduction of the postal vote. The tendency is for the existing machine to select the new general secretary or president and then ensure he is elected. Thus oligarchy perpetuates itself.

The actual number who vote in vital union elections is usually well under 50 per cent, the great majority of them from the big branches which are easier for the union bureaucracy to control. When Jack Jones was General Secretary of the Transport and General Workers Union, he was, according to an opinion poll, rated 'the most powerful man in Britain'. But out of 1,418,140 members, only 529,546 or 37 per cent voted at his election; and Jones got 334,125 of these — less than a quarter of the members in fact. His successor, the present General Secretary, Moss

Evans, was elected by less than half of a 39 per cent poll — one fifth of the members. David Basnett, elected General Secretary of the General and Municipal Workers' Union for life, was the beneficiary of the union's 'block' branch ballot system — the candidate who gets the majority of the votes of those attending the branch meeting is credited with all the votes of its members. Officially, then, nearly ninety per cent of the branches voted. But the number of individual members who actually voted was perhaps less than ten per cent.

Introduction of postal ballots certainly helps — but not as much as one might suppose. When Hugh Scanlon was elected as the left-wing candidate for President of the Engineers' Union, only eleven per cent of members voted. Subsequent introduction of postal balloting raised the total to 38 per cent, and the left-wing candidate lost. But this does not mean that the members get what they want. Although Mr Terry Duffy, the present 'moderate' President of the union, and the General Secretary, Sir John Boyd, were elected by postal ballot, they have to carry out policy — including the recent one- and two-day strikes — decided by the 52 members of the rank-and-file National Committee. In 1979 this National Committee had a majority of two for the communists and fellow-travellers and instructed its top officials accordingly. The key meetings at which these men were elected were sometimes attended by as few as eight or nine trade union members.

Such is some indication of the slender popular basis, in terms of actual live people, on which the 'Democracy of the Committed' rests — a few thousand active members of the Labour party, a few thousand militant trade unionists. Yet the changes in the way the Labour party is run will place this elite oligarchy, many of whom do not subscribe to the principles of parliamentary democracy at all, in a position to mandate Labour MPs and instruct a Labour Cabinet.

Let me point out that we are already suffering from what Lord Hailsham has called 'elective dictatorship', for we have no written constitution in Britain and, in theory, Parliament is absolutely sovereign. In the last Parliament, the governing party had been chosen by only 29 per cent of the electorate but it enacted some very repressive and obnoxious acts, such as the Industrial Relations Acts of 1974 and 1976, the Employment Protection Act of 1975 and a particularly objectionable Rent Act; various Finance Bills enormously increased the right of search and entry enjoyed by government officials. We have to face the fact that the notion of unrestricted parliamentary sovereignty exposes us to the possibility that our fundamental rights and freedoms can at any time be abolished or reduced by a Parliament which acknowledges no concept of fundamental or unalterable law but acts by simple majority, conceivably consisting of a minority of Members of Parliament as a whole, representing a minority of popular votes, and acting upon the command of a National Executive or local party executives which are controlled in practice by very few people indeed – and people whose policies are orchestrated from behind the scenes.

Of course, in the last resort, the vote of the electorate is decisive. Karl Popper has rightly suggested that the essence of democracy is not 'one man one vote' – that may be, and often is, worthless – but the right to dismiss a government. Democracy means accountability. But does the 'Democracy of the Committed' mean accountability? I rather think not. I am particularly concerned by the curious interest that the totalitarian Left of the Labour party displays in the House of Lords. This has cropped up time and again in the internal rows of the party. Why? One clue, I think, is provided by the last Labour party manifesto. It reads: 'We propose, therefore, in the next parliament to abolish the delaying power and legislative veto of the House of Lords'. What is the meaning of the phrase 'legislative veto of the House of Lords'? Has the House of Lords a legislative veto, one may ask? The answer lies in the Parliament Act of 1911, Section 2, which deprives the Lords of their veto power, but specifically excepts 'a Bill containing any provision to extend the maximum duration of Parliament beyond five years'. This provision endorsed by the 1949 Parliament Act, is the only instance in which the Lords retain a veto. Hence. the insertion of those three words 'and legislative veto' was intended and *can only* have been intended to clear the way to give a Labour-controlled Commons the right to extend its own life indefinitely.

The Parliament Act of 1911 was a temporary act, enacted pending further legislation about an elective second chamber. This is often overlooked. Hence, in coming to the third question I asked at the beginning – what steps can we take to avert the threat to democracy? – I think we might begin by pressing for the completion of the unfinished business of the 1911 Act and bring into existence a reformed and authoritative second chamber while the opportunity still exists. This second chamber should be designed to curb the notion of one-chamber unlimited sovereignty, by investing residual powers, of a custodial nature, in a second chamber with an unassailable popular base and one that is not susceptible to the 'creation of peers' technique.

A second line of defence against 'elective dictatorship' is to enact a Bill of Rights. For all practical purposes, the proposal is that a Bill based upon the European Convention for the Protection of Human Rights and Fundamental Freedoms should be enacted by Parliament so that this Convention will operate at every level of the judicial process. At present under a 1966 agreement, British subjects can apply to the Human Rights Commission for relief only when they have exhausted local remedies — as in the thalidomide case, where a House of Lords ruling was overthrown. By enacting a Bill of Rights we would counter 'elective dictatorship' by establishing a procedure by which oppressive statutes might be invalidated. It is true that no Parliament can bind its successor; but I would argue that a Bill of Rights, passed by Parliament and endorsed by referendum, might well be upheld by the courts as superior to any subsequent statute of an ordinary kind. In any event, it could constitute an indelible marker or Rubicon, the crossing of which would constitute the manifest transition from constitutionalism to tyranny.

There is a third possibility which ought to be considered and which I think will be increasingly canvassed as the contest for power within the Labour party intensifies. There have always been strong objections to the notion of a political party being financed by interest groups, whether by trade unions on the one hand, or big business on the other. In some European countries, a system has been introduced whereby the parties are subsidized from the public purse on the basis of electoral performances — that is, the number of parliamentary seats they hold. There are, of course, many obvious objections to this system. Hitherto, the British Conservative party has rejected the possibility completely, not only on the general grounds that it marks a further extension of state subsidy, but on the particular grounds that it destroys the dynamism of the political process. The Labour party has been more sympathetic to the notion, though for different and sometimes conflicting reasons. We may soon, however, face a realignment of views on this issue. If a chasm opens between the totalitarian elements in the Labour party, controlling the party machine and executive, and therefore the source of finance (and most of the local parties) on the one hand, and the great majority of serving Labour MPs on the other, it may well be in the national interest for the state to intervene on the side of the social democratic element and provide an alternative source of finance. This is the kind of argument which would have a strong appeal to a Conservative government — and, needless to say, to the bulk of Labour MPs, who are attached to the democratic process in its parliamentary form and wish to maintain it.

In conclusion, there is considerable evidence of anti-democratic tendencies at work within both the Labour party and the trade union movement. And those tendencies are likely to grow stronger. But there are precise measures which can be taken to counter such tendencies, and in my view these are likely to become topics of active debate in the very near future.

CHAPTER FOUR

Italian Political Parties and Italian Society

ARRIGO LEVI

The Crisis of Democracies and the 'Italian Case'

In recent years a wide and passionate debate has been going on in the West about 'the crisis of democracies', the emerging consensus being that there was indeed a decline in the governability of democracies, a fall in social discipline, a decline in respect for the law, and an increase in social tensions and demands. The result of this was to make the task of democratic governments increasingly difficult. The democratic ideals of general prosperity, social equality, freedom of the individual and political participation have led to an unprecedented expansion of the functions of governments everywhere. But any achievements could never match expectations, and great tensions arose everywhere among the Western nations. However, considerable differences among them reflect on the degree to which the phenomenon of ungovernability has progressed.

Some national political systems appeared to be under greater stress and looked less capable of standing up to the trials of our age. The Italian case was considered to be among those that were critical. Although West Germany appears to be psychologically insecure and Britain

economically unstable, most of the Western nations
appear to be secure institutionally and to be stable socially
and economically. Italy, although often described as vital
and growing, has also been described as both unstable and
insecure. It is also described as being a society with some
new species of acrobatic democracy, which by some
mysterious trick has been able to find a way out of
impossible problems. Another contradiction rests in the
unequalled degree of political continuity. Italy is unstable,
but it has been ruled for the last three decades by one
party, Christian Democracy – and friends.

As a result of these curious features and the dramatic
qualities inherent in Italian life, the 'Italian case' has
attracted an unusual degree of attention. Reports by
foreign observers are sometimes puzzled, more often
dramatic: sometimes it's 'Italy in turmoil', sometimes even
'Italy in agony'. Italians cannot resent some
simplifications by foreign observers: discussing the Italian
case, and presenting it as a tragedy rather than as a
'commedia dell'arte', has become the Italians' national
hobby.

But why does the case-history of Italian democracy
appear to be particularly serious? Prima facie evidence
includes a list of relevant facts, for example terrorism,
social unrest and mass violence, very high inflation, and
continuous strikes. A party which was originally anti-
democratic, the Italian Communist party (PCI), remains
very strong and new revolutionary ideologies show
unexpected vitality. Government crises are frequent and
ever longer. 'Ungovernability' means in Italy not a vague
social disease but the absence of majority government as a
recurring condition which has already twice led to the
premature ending of a legislature.

While Italian bureaucracy is notorious, corruption is
widespread in public life and the Mafia and organized
crime are stronger than ever. In one way or another all

these aspects of the Italian case are considered to be related. Italy's political parties appear to be unable to offer solutions to these problems, and their prestige, at least that of the traditional, 'historical' parties, has never sunk so low as in recent years. All this leads to the question often being asked — will Italian democracy survive?

Italy as a Late Developer

Just as the crisis of Western democracy is often described as arising out of the explosive growth of democracy since the war, it is usually observed that the Italian crisis is connected with modernization and an unprecedented process of economic, social and cultural growth which has made the last few decades of Italian history a period as creative and vital as any in the past. If this is an unstable society, it certainly is not a dull and stagnant one. Italy's contribution to the development of cultural-political trends of worldwide significance and impact has been a relevant one, including the 'aggiornamento' of the Catholic Church and that other 'aggiornamento' which is called — whatever its real values — Eurocommunism, Rome being the undisputed capital of both movements.

The obvious indicators of the vitality of this frontier country of the West are, in mysterious and subtle ways, connected to the crisis indicators. In today's Italy the human condition reaches moments of great feverish and creative vitality. Just one step beyond, drama, even tragedy, are waiting. These are times of great troubles, but the passions, values and ideals that stand behind them are not vulgar and puny. This is, as Peter Lange once put it, a 'mobilized' society, engaged in a vital, unending debate about problems of justice and democracy which are not of purely Italian relevance.

The Italians face today's problem carrying with them a

difficult and complex inheritance. Italy's contemporary democracy was born out of a genuine popular revolt against Fascism. But Fascism was itself a genuine Italian mass political movement. Italy invented Fascism, the original model for many governments sharing its authoritarian, totalitarian, demagogic characteristics. Many late-developing nations are, even today, ruled by governments of a Fascist type. Just as unusual in the West, Italy's Left early acquired some of the typical features of the revolutionary Left of Eastern Europe. Although communism and Fascism were present elsewhere in the West, nowhere else were such a powerful Fascist bourgeois movement and an equally powerful communist proletarian movement present in the same nation during the period of just one generation.

In comparison with the rest of Western Europe, the Italian Republic received from its past, together with this unattractive historical inheritance, a condition of definite economic-social backwardness. Italy was less heavily industrialized and urbanized and had a far larger agricultural population and stronger social and regional diversities than any other Western European democracy at the end of the last war. In remembering those years one wonders how it could be that, in spite of everything, our hopes for a better future were so strong.

Italy's democratic leaders and thinkers shared then a widespread belief that 'the achievement of economic growth was the great problem for [all] European nations: if only our GNP could grow for long enough, most of our troubles as divided and nonconsensual politics would gradually disappear' (I quote from the report by the Trilateral Commission on the 'crisis of democracies', a passage which does not refer to Italy but to the whole of Europe). Today, having learnt many bitter lessons, we have reached the conclusion that economic progress is indeed a precondition for political stability and the growth of democracy, but is not sufficient in itself to make democratic societies strong and secure. We have become aware of the fact that economic progress and modernization are complicated processes, and they may even be the source of many of our present difficulties. This was particularly true of a 'late developer' like Italy.

Modernization and Social Conflict

Thanks to the great variety of our experiences in various cultural and geographical environments, we are now well aware of the fact that modernization may be a good thing, but is bound to bring about great structural and psychological changes which usually produce great political instability. Such phenomena are stronger in countries of delayed development as compared with their regional environment, and this is the case of Italy. Economic development is often very uneven; some geographical areas, some social sectors of the population, may be involved in a furious process of modernization while other areas and sectors may still be untouched by them. It then happens that the more advanced areas tend to absorb a disproportionate amount of national resources. There is little doubt that participation in the Common Market, while being a very powerful factor in the modernization of Italy (the 'Italian miracle'), tended to further strengthen this phenomenon. The advanced areas, mostly in the industrialized North, imitated and equalled the standard of living, the wages and 'consumption model' of our more developed European partners. The backward areas of our economy and society, which are mostly in the South, were relatively deprived of their share of resources. Inequalities tended to increase rather than diminish. The great efforts of the Italian state to direct resources towards the backward areas of society were as unsatisfactory as the labour of Sisyphus.

Meanwhile, the demand for equality became stronger. During the last three decades a powerful national process of cultural and social unification has destroyed many of our traditional class differences and barriers. A massive movement of population from the country to the cities, from the South to the North, as well as the spread of universal education and television, have for the first time in our history laid the foundation for a unified Italian society, speaking the same language, rather than dialects, and sharing the same ideals and way of life. Old and new injustices seemed unbearable when they clashed with the new demands for universal prosperity and equality, which are the promises of democracy, as well as with some considerable but partial achievements.

One must also remember that there existed among the components of Italy's collective identity powerful elements of millenarian ideology of both Catholic and Marxist extraction. The Communist party continued preaching a revolutionary gospel until relatively recent times, which left a powerful imprint on the minds of the young, even after the Communist party started to pour a lot of water into the strong wine of revolution. Great expectations, together with the strong remnants of old class hates, old and new injustices, and revolutionary ideologies, were powerful ingredients for a very explosive mixture.

In such a highly competitive, impatient and ambitious society, pressure groups of all kinds came to feel that only by increasing the level of social tension and conflict could they obtain adequate attention and at least partial satisfaction of their demands by an 'overloaded' and inefficient state. Italy became an ever more 'conflictual' society, but the very growth of social conflict, the fall in political consent, the decline of cooperative attitudes in social institutions and economic enterprises, the crisis of authority, reduced the capacity for growth. Resources were inadequate for development, and what had to be urgently consumed today could not be invested for a better future. Social demands became ever more impatient and destructive. Inflation is only the most visible indicator of this tendency to overconsume and is a yardstick of the growing gap between expectations and the resources actually available to satisfy them. It is also a highly destabilizing social and economic factor in itself. And so we saw the vicious circle of antisocial behaviour and a decline in economic efficiency.

In a democracy when antisocial behaviour becomes widespread, the political institutions whose job it is to enforce the law find themselves facing a painful dilemma. They have either to use force, which is in itself repugnant to the democratic way of life, or to submit to the arrogance of anarchic power, or to try to mediate and compromise. The result may well be a gradual decline in the quality of life and respect for the law, but in time much worse things can happen.

Of course, similar patterns of antisocial behaviour and conflict can easily be found elsewhere in the West. As we have already found, the 'crisis of democracy' is not purely Italian. But the Italian crisis has special features which are not found elsewhere and which reveal some deep weaknesses of our democracy. Two such features are the unsolved problem of the Communist party – of its evolution and full participation in political life – and the rise of new extremist revolutionary factions and the wave of terrorism. The crisis of Italy's political parties and Italian democracy often appear as a background to these acute problems.

The Communist Problem

Opinions about the Italian Communist party vary greatly. Some people firmly believe that a Communist party may change its tactics and appearance but not its real identity and long-term aims, which remain the conquest and totalitarian exercise of power. The PCI, according to this view, is quite good at imitating democratic behaviour in order to gain recognition and legitimation as a bona fide democratic party, but it has not really changed its original allegiance to Soviet communism. Indeed, if it came to power, it would quickly betray its promises and set up a communist totalitarian state.

Other people, mostly on the extreme Left, have convinced themselves that the Italian Communist party is communist only by name, that it has changed its real identity and policies, so that it is today a social democratic party with no intention whatsoever of making a revolution. It continues to call itself communist in order to better deceive the proletariat and lead them along the path of moderation.

A third body of opinion holds that the Communist party is undergoing a genuine process of change which involves its identity, ideology and policies. But such a process is rich in contradictions; the identity of the party is still uncertain and one cannot tell for sure how it will develop or even whether recent trends will not be reversed. The Communist party should therefore be considered as 'on probation', and should not be granted full recognition as a normal democratic party, to the point, for example, of being accepted as a full partner in government.

Although probably the majority of observers in Italy belong to this third school of thought, it is important to recognize that responsible opinion is still divided and is continuously changing. Clarifying what the Communist party is may be even less important than assessing what it is thought to be. Different people see it differently, and most have been changing their minds about it. Even worse, it can be easily shown that the Communist party itself is uncertain about its own identity, which makes it less surprising that this identity should be unclear to others and a subject of continuing debate. The fact that Italy's second largest party, representing about a third of the electorate, should have this uncertain and contradictory nature and should be seen so differently by different people, is in itself very unsettling.

Of all the strange features of the Italian situation, this could very well be the strangest. For this huge and successful Communist party, which contrives to look communist to some and democratic to others, with both judgements being equally sincere, is indeed a strange and new feature.

It is, of course, difficult to have to deal with an object which looks so different to different people. But a large and even increasing body of people recognize themselves in this 'mysterious' object and vote for it. The PCI may be strange but it certainly exists and it is an essential part of the Italian scenery. Beyond the almost metaphysical problem of its identity, we know it well – its faults and qualities, dedication and duplicity, ambiguities and sincere torments. In some way we recognize in the uniquely troubled identity of the Italian Communist party, uneasily balancing itself between East and West, the troubled and equally unique identity of our own country and people, a frontier nation if ever there was one. But a frontier region of the West, not between East and West, a marginal country of the democratic world.

This is said in order to create a better awareness of the extraordinary problems faced by Italy's traditional democratic parties. The Christian Democrats, Liberals, Socialists, Social Democrats and Republicans all are at present engaged in defining their difficult relations with the PCI, hoping for various and varying types of cooperation in the business of governing the country, and even today, with the Communist party again 'in the opposition', strong elements of the policy of '*solidarità nazionale*' remain in existence, in Parliament, local government, and in various public enterprises and corporations. Many would still argue with Moro's view that at the present time, in order to create an area of political consensus wide enough to make Italy 'governable', some degree of cooperation with the PCI must be envisaged, and is, for some time at least, necessary.

But if one bears in mind what the PCI is today as against what it was, the present difficulties in forming a stable political majority in Italy do not appear to be due to some strange feature of our political/electoral system, nor to the stupidity of politicians, but instead to real problems, deeply connected with the troubled identity of our nation, and to the tensions existing inside our society. Indeed, our divided democratic system embodies and represents only too well the real image of our country.

To Italian political observers it is also apparent that the political elites in all parties are probably nearer to each other than the parties themselves, or even their separate bodies of electors. One often feels that the parties and party leaders have been doing all they can in order to aggregate and make governable a genuinely and deeply divided society. Their success is only partial.

If this analysis is at all correct in trying to shift at least part of the blame for Italy's ungovernability from the political parties, who are usually identified as 'the culprits', to Italian democracy, a solution will not be reached either easily or soon thanks to some political trick. Italy's 'normalization' as a democracy still depends upon deeper and far-reaching changes in the nature, not just of political parties such as the PCI, but of Italian society. Until such changes take place, it is difficult to imagine the coming into existence of a normal political consent between Italy's political institutions as exists elsewhere in older and more stable democracies. It is equally difficult to imagine the emergence of a genuine historical compromise as it has existed for a long time in those democratic countries where opposite parties and classes easily tolerate the electoral victory of their political opponents.

The Rise of Terrorism

Some observers feel that the Communist party has been doubly responsible for the rise of an extremist, revolutionary and terrorist movement in Italy in the 1970s. First, by keeping alive for a long time the myth of Leninist revolution, and second, for later betraying that myth and commitment and gradually acquiring the image, if not the full identity, of a non-revolutionary party of the Left. It has been said by the former Communist Rossana Rossanda that Italy's extra-parliamentary Left, including the terrorist groups, use the 'family Lexicon' of old communism, and this is difficult to deny.

Historical responsibility for the rise of a terrorist movement in Italy cannot however be laid entirely at the door of the PCI. Were not the parties in control of Italy's governments since the war, most of all the Christian Democrats, the real culprits? Was it not their fault if social and economic conditions arose that favoured the development of terrorism? If the prestige of the state has fallen into disrepute and its authority has decayed, can it not be said that these are the consequences of serious mistakes in planning the development of the economy and of the lack of foresight in anticipating the social consequences of growth?

The parties so long in power, most of all the Christian Democrats, came to feel that they 'owned' the state, and they behaved as a '*razza padrona*', a master race. Hence the cases of corruption and the continuous widening of the public sector of the economy and its increasing exploitation by the dominating political parties for purposes of power and enrichment and for political protection.

The years of the rise of the new extra-parliamentary opposition, of new powerful political movements and even new parties such as the Radicals, were also the years — the early 1970s — when Christian Democracy was subjected to a great national trial through the mass media and political debate as well as through a flood of books and pamphlets. Not just Christian Democracy but the whole of '*il Palazzo*' (the Palace or Establishment), as Pasolini called it, was on trial. There were also actual trials for corruption in which the highest personalities were involved, with even the resignation of a President of the Republic, probably guilty only of associating with the wrong people, and the condemnation of a former secretary general of the Social Democratic party in the Lockheed scandal.

To some extent this nationwide trial was a substitute for that normal feature of most democracies, the winning of an election by the former opposition parties and a total change in government. While the electoral consequences of the trial were quite marked in the 1976 elections, which opened the door to the Communist party joining new government majorities, there was no radical change of the kind which takes place when a party is condemned by the electorate to leave government power and move to the opposition benches. Such changes only took place in Italy in local government. As far as the central government was concerned, Christian Democrats and Communists were forced by an indecisive verdict into a difficult political embrace.

To many young people it must have seemed clear that the electoral process by itself would never be able to force real change in Italy's political life. The Communists themselves were seen as traitors to the ideal of revolution and change. This contributed to the rise of an antiparliamentary mentality among the young. The new revolutionary ideals which spread among the young in the late 1960s and early 1970s in various countries of the Western world found in Italy a particularly favourable terrain. Gradually the use of political violence in various institutions, not only the universities but even in some of the biggest factories of the North, led to the creation of genuine terrorist organizations, of which the Red Brigades are only the better known.

While terrorism emerged from the students' movement of the late 1960s, it is not yet possible to say when, or even if, it will come to an end. In the history of terrorist movements there often comes a moment when the original political aims shared by at least one section of society, either of a national or social and ideological character, seem to be forgotten or become less important. Then terrorism becomes an end in itself, and although it may remain active for quite some time, terrorists find themselves increasingly isolated from the rest of society. Sooner or later they can be uprooted and destroyed. Italian terrorism, which has proved totally unable to act as the 'detonator of Revolution', may be going along this path. But the end has not been reached and terrorism is not yet totally isolated; the area of confused sympathies and even complicity remains uncomfortably large.

The strategy adopted by the political forces in order to combat terrorism was on the whole a soft strategy, and deliberately so. The measures taken against terrorism remain well within the limits of what is consistent with the tolerant rules of democratic life. An expert like Professor Walter Laqueur believes that this proves that we must not exaggerate the seriousness of the terrorist danger in Italy. He once told me:

The fact that Italy has not adopted extreme measures against terrorism is very significant. If terrorism had been felt to be a mortal danger for civil life, there would have been no hesitation in adopting the harshest possible measures; societies are always ready to adopt them in order to defend themselves, even if this means sacrificing democracy. In Italy this has not happened: it confirms my belief that we have always overestimated the political importance of terrorism.

The choice of a soft strategy, which includes, for example, allowing the free publication of a number of daily newspapers regularly preaching the cause of revolution and violence, was a deliberate one and not just a result of weakness. The view of successive Italian governments was that an overreaction to terrorism might be fatal and play into the hands of the terrorists. Many observers, while on the whole approving this soft strategy, felt for a long time that a share of the responsibility for the rise of terrorism in Italy fell upon the persistent weakness of Italy's democratic authorities. This included the men responsible for such institutions as the universities in the late 1960s with their widespread and contagious explosions of anarchic and violent behaviour. If the arrogance of the violent minorities had been met with greater firmness from the very beginning, the practice of violence would have been checked and the qualitative jump into terrorism, which took place around the middle of the 1970s, might have been prevented or at least kept within narrower limits. But the continuum of violence was not broken and the timidity of authority made the enemies of law and order more and more daring and ambitious.

However, terrorism had a beginning and it is not irrational to believe that it will also have an end. Some signs of the beginning of the end seem to be apparent right now, although we cannot be sure yet that this story is reaching its final chapter.

The Crisis and the Parties

In trying to analyse the reasons for the crisis of Italian democracy in the 1970s I have stressed two aspects: the socio-economic conditions connected with Italy's being a late developer and the political conditions, in particular the special problem of Italy's Communist party. That special anomaly of our democracy which consists in its *'bipartitismo imperfetto'*, its being an imperfect two-party system where there is never a change in government, is a direct consequence of the separateness and diversity of the PCI, qualities which even recent speeches by Mr Berlinguer insistently reaffirm.

I do not want to give the impression, by trying to provide an all-inclusive, coherent picture of the Italian case, that this picture is static and unchanging. I think that there was a clearly recognizable turning point in the evolution of the Italian crisis, a moment when things suddenly began getting worse and hopes for a gradual improvement of our social conflicts dramatically fell. The turning point came about mostly as a result of events which had nothing to do with Italy. In the summer of 1973 a new and ambitious Centre-Left coalition had been formed, the Rumor government, in which the management of economic policy as well as of social and economic reforms had been put into the hands of the so-called 'troika' of economic ministers, Colombo, La Malfa and Giolitti. Much was expected from them. Then in the autumn the sudden outbreak of the oil crisis totally upset the government's plans and imposed harsh deflationary measures.

From that moment on, social tensions quickly increased to an explosive level and our crisis, which was until then physiological, became pathological. In the following years a series of unstable coalition governments succeeded in saving Italy from bankruptcy by adopting policies of unexpected severity. But this had disruptive political consequences. The end of the Centre-Left era of governments based on the Christian Democrat-Socialist alliance, the sudden strengthening of the Communist party, the explosive rise in inflation and unemployment, and finally the spread of violence and terrorism, all these were the indirect consequences of the great economic crisis of the West that followed the somewhat accidental oil crisis in 1973. Only then, I believe, did the Italian case become such a source of anxiety to Italy's friends in the world, and serious doubts arose about the governability of Italian democracy.

What made our crisis so serious were the structural weaknesses of our society and the political mistakes of our parties. But the crisis in its acute form had a beginning and may be expected to have an end, although we are not sure that it is near or even that it will be a favourable one for all concerned. In my view, the crisis itself has shown that Italian society is not passive but reacts to it and can perhaps overcome it completely.

There are various signs of this capacity to react. In the economic field, the spontaneous qualities of our workers and entrepreneurs are behind the remarkable recovery of our foreign balances. The remarkable growth of a parallel economy, which partly coincides with a proliferation of activities by small firms, shows the resilience of a spontaneous capitalist mentality which is typically Italian. In the political sphere the necessary degree of cooperation between parties who had long been fierce enemies made the acceptance of severe deflationary policies possible. The unity of Italian society behind the democratic ideals which are identified in the Republic, born of the Resistance, was repeatedly demonstrated in times of great psychological stress. Italy's public opinion and political leaders of all parties were united and uncompromising in their refusal of the terrorists's blackmail during the tragic days of the

Moro kidnapping. Never were Italy's weaknesses so apparent as in those days, but they also showed that no political alternative to the Republic was in sight and that the Republic still had reserves of strength which could save it.

During those years Italy's political life became extraordinarily lively. Great debates and referendums took place on such matters as divorce, increased powers for the police, the public financing of political parties, and abortion, and usually the more modern views prevailed. New forms of participatory democracy were devised in the schools and the regions. The Italy of these years was indeed the country of debates, and where the traditional parties failed new movements appeared, often demagogic but stimulating. These were dangerous critical years and yet we had the feeling, in suffering every single critical moment as if it might be the last, that these were creative years and if we were able to overcome our crisis, our democracy would become a better and healthier political society than it had ever been. The relationship between the general public and the political parties became quite aggressive and demanding. The press and television opened up to unprecedentedly drastic discussions on public affairs and public figures.

The main result in political terms was a much greater flexibility among the electorate. The sharp increase in the Communist vote in 1976 and the almost equally sharp decline in support for the PCI in the 1979 elections proved that a floating vote had come into existence in Italy for the first time. A substantial body of voters could move right across the political spectrum from one party to the other and back as happens in normal democracies. Our society became less polarized, less divided. This makes the task of our politicians more difficult and demanding, which is not a bad thing, but the spell has not been broken and we are not yet able to produce either an alternation in the holding of power by political parties or a full-scale national coalition to counteract what is widely recognized as a national emergency.

The Search Continues

There is still some terrorism and still an abnormal level of social conflict. There is still an unstable political system where government by coalition with all its usual faults – lack of decisiveness, sluggish compromises, contradictory choices – is the only possibility. But even coalitions are unstable, and recently the country has remained for many months without a majority government. So we are not yet out of our crisis, and the usual explanation of it is that it is all the fault of the politicians. Undoubtedly our political elite has been guilty of arrogance, selfishness, lack of vision, reluctance to change, but having myself so often and so harshly criticized our politicians, let me say that I consider it foolish to ignore the objective, structural reasons for the tensions and conflicts which make Italy almost ungovernable.

This is a stiff-necked people who are difficult to govern. Although the country is less deeply divided than it was – and partly as a result of that – it is still incapable, except in moments of great danger, of producing an adequate level of political-social consent, which older and more stable democracies can do. With all their faults, our politicians can be credited with the one virtue of patience. Without the patient tolerance of one another on the part of Italy's main political party leaders perhaps our crisis would already have reached an explosive level more than once. If there is no clear majority in the Italian Parliament, and there has not been one for some years, this is not the politicians' fault. Even at the last elections the three main parties – Christian Democrats, Communists and

Socialists − offered a clear choice to the electors. These offers were all refused and no clear majority emerged either for a new Centre, a new Centre-Left, or a new Left majority. The politicians can only make the best of an objectively unmanageable situation.

Looking at the recent past I believe that it was wise for Italy's non-Communist parties to adopt a soft approach to the problem of their relations with the PCI. A certain degree of association with the PCI was, and to some extent still is, considered necessary, not because the Christian Democrats and others foolishly ignored the risks of such a course, but because the necessary level of cooperation in an emergency could not be obtained otherwise, and the results were not irrelevant. Large sectors of Italian society may not be able to establish normal relations with the state until they have a feeling that this is 'their' state, which they have had a share in running. Just imagine what the crisis would be like in Britain if the Labour party had never been in government. A normalization of the diffident relationship prevailing between state and citizen in Italy may have to wait until all classes of society and all sectors of political opinion have had a taste of government, including the Communists and their electorate. We are all clearly aware of how dangerous this process is going to be, but I do not think that anything that has happened so far justifies lack of confidence in the caution and sense of responsibility of the leaderships of Italy's traditional democratic parties in dealing with this arduous task. For whatever share the Communists have had in recent years in government responsibilities, it has so far mostly contributed to making Italy less ungovernable.

Looking at the future, the fact that the last elections have so dramatically interrupted the unbroken ascent of the Communist party while denying the Christian Democrats that vote of confidence for which they hoped, has left the situation open to many new developments. It appears that the period of national solidarity has left its imprint on Italy's political society in the sense that relations between the Communist party and the other parties continue to be more relaxed and cooperative than they were before and that some historical compromise may still be in existence. But other parties feel that they may have a chance to obtain greater support. The new activism of such traditional parties as the Socialists, Liberals and Social Democrats, the rise of new personalities inside the Christian Democratic party, the greater influence of the President of the Republic, and the discussion of the possibility of institutional reforms, all these are pointers to possibly great changes in a political situation which appeared to be either paralysed or moving just in one direction, namely towards an increase in the power of the Communist party.

Sometimes history changes the subject, and Italy's Communists may still miss the bus of history while other parties may jump on it. In the wider European framework the democratic parties of the Left, in particular the socialists, appear to be capable of gaining strength. Within that framework the Communist party will be submitted to pressures aiming at its Westernization.

The strengthening and development of European institutions remains a top priority on our agenda for economic and political reasons. The same can be said for the achievement of a more stable international economic environment through the control of disruptive inflation. We received a deep wound from the international economic crisis, and I do not know how many more we can afford. Most analyses of the Italian case end by reminding us of the importance of further progress towards the unification of Europe and the strengthening of the Atlantic world, and I shall make no excuses for doing the same.

CHAPTER FIVE

The Crisis of the Italian Political System and the Elections of June 1979

GIUSEPPE ARE

The Italian Communist party (PCI) received basic recognition of its legitimacy during the legislature which began with its great advance in the 1976 elections. It was in fact regarded as a necessary member of the majorities of national unity and deemed capable of providing an irreplaceable contribution to the solution of the Italian crisis. However, during 1978 it became quite clear that this political formula, which had been stubbornly demanded and prepared for by the PCI, was not functioning according to the timetable envisaged. Its claim to become a full member of the government, although supported by other parties, was intransigently rejected by the Christian Democrats (DC), essentially for fear that it might lead to mass defections among its own traditional supporters at the polls. The PCI found itself barred from the most important stage of the extension and consolidation of its influence on Italian politics, precisely when both its old and new supporters were showing signs of impatience and disappointment. It therefore came to see early elections as the best way of overcoming this obstacle.

Taken as the expression of the will of the Italian people,

the general election of 3 June 1979, and even more so the European election of 10 June, comprised a severe setback to this grand design of the PCI, comparable only to that suffered on 18 April 1948. And this is not just because of the numbers of votes lost compared with the previous two stages of its great leap forward (1975 and 1976) but because analysis shows that it is even more a setback in terms of the changes, in many ways substantial, in the balance of forces on which the Communist party's strategy was relying. The first figures in table 5.1 are startling, for not only was it the first time that the party had lost votes in any general election since 1946, but the losses were heavy. Compared with 1976, the percentage points lost in the general election and in the lower poll in the European elections mean that the PCI lost 12 per cent of its 1976 support in the former and 14 per cent in the latter. However, compared with 1972

TABLE 5.1 Electoral trends: the PCI, the Left and the DC from 1946 to 1949

Year	1946	1948	1953	1958	1963	1968	1972	1976	1979	1979 European
Percentage of votes for the Left*	39.2	31	35.3	36.9	39.1	41.2	38.8	46.6	45.8	46.1
Variations of the Left		−8.6	+4.3	+1.6	+2.2	+2.1	−2.6	+8	−0.8	+0.3
Percentage of votes for the PCI	18.9	21	22.6	22.7	25.3	26.9	27.1	34.4	30.4	29.6
Proportion of PCI votes in the total for the Left	47.7	–	64	61.5	64.7	65.2	70.2	73.8	66.3	64.1
Percentage of votes for the DC	35,2	48.5	40.1	42.4	38.3	39.1	38.7	38.8	38.3	36.5
Percentage of votes for the DC in the North and Centre in the latest elections								North 38.9	North 37.1	North West 34.4
										North East 36.7
								Centre 34.2	Centre 33.9	Centre 31.7

* The Left comprises: PCI, PSI, Radicals and two small extremist parties, Democrazia Proletaria (DP) and Partito di Unità Proletaria (PDUP).

it gained 12 per cent in the general election, equivalent to 6 per cent per election for the two held since then, a slower rate of growth than for the period 1958 to 1963 but equal to that for 1963-68.

The significance of these data is that the special factors of the PCI's cyclical growth during the last decade have ceased, and indeed an inverse trend has now begun. The party has fallen back on its long-term growth, which is gradual and very slow, as between 1946 and 1972. This slow growth might appear comforting to its leaders and their approach to politics, were it not an indication of difficulties which make a linear trend in the domestic and international political situation seem highly unlikely. For such a trend was the background to the slow and gradual growth of Communist support in the 1950s and 1960s. For example, as with its defeat at the polls, there came a drop in the recruitment figures for the Young Communists, which began in 1977 and became disastrous in 1978. Again, similar downward trends for the party itself can no longer be regarded as resulting from their occasional organizational lapses and inefficiency.

Given the highly efficient organization of the Communist machine, and that the gains achieved in both votes and membership between 1975 and 1976 went hand in hand, the setback, though subject to confirmation by events, may be seen as a new cycle of decline. Likewise, the duration of this decline in making new converts for the party, although difficult to predict, promises to have quite a different character from the cycle which lasted from 1955 to 1971. At that time the fall in membership (from 2,145,000 to 1,574,000) did not prevent a gradual rise in electoral support for the party, indeed both phenomena occurred simultaneously throughout the period. This time, however, it is accompanied by a fall in support at the polls, which is already very substantial and unprecedented from the quantitative point of view, but is a veritable catastrophe in the obstacle it presents to the prosecution of the strategies and to the pursuit of the goals to which the PCI was utterly committed.

Thus the PCI has been badly mauled on the very front where it had most boldly claimed to be advancing during the 1970s, i.e. the electoral front where the party believed it could aggregate the political demands of highly diversified social forces and act upon political decision-making processes through the sheer numbers of its supporters and their influence in representative institutions. However, it is clear that for the first time its organizational structure was not able to consolidate its previous electoral successes, convey persuasively the party's messages to all the supporters previously won over, nor achieve their permanent embracement of its political goals. This inadequacy and failure are the sign of a turning-point in the overall evolution of the PCI and its relations with Italian society. They are in fact a sign that, in the context of traumatic changes in the country's domestic social arrangements and its international environment, the traditional methods of bureaucratic regimentation and ideological indoctrination are incapable of compensating, beyond a certain limit, for the lack or ambiguity of basic policies or definitions about its medium- and long-term aims. To put it simply, in a society which has unequivocally become much more dynamic, pluralistic, informed and free than in the 1960s and 1950s, *organization* alone no longer suffices to maintain the PCI's position if its policy is, or is perceived as being, ambiguous, contradictory, dangerous, or in any way inadequate to meet the country's problems.

Of even greater importance, however, are the data relating to the system of political kinships within which the PCI has to work. Firstly, even the total overall percentage of votes for the Left has dropped, falling noticeably shorter of 50 per cent in the national general election than in the European poll. This means that its bargaining power and its representativeness would decline even on the hypothesis that all its components were akin to the PCI and prepared to accept its dominance or to follow its lead. However, this hypothesis as never been so far from fulfilment since 1946 as it is today. In particular, the PCI today has far less claim to expect or impose such a supremacy. Here too, in contrast with a steady, unbroken trend since 1946, the proportion of PCI votes within those of the Left as a whole has not only fallen compared with previous elections, but plunged even lower in the European election.

Apart from the figures, however, it is the nature and culture of this Left which have changed profoundly. Even the PDUP, the component of the Left which is closest to the PCI, and which can be regarded as a kind of external faction of it, derives its own justification and identity from its attempts to confront and upset the PCI's plan to reach an understanding with the Christian Democrats. The Communist leadership still clings to this plan, the PDUP's ambition being to become the real leader and intellect of an alternative strategy of left-wing unity which may finally replace the PCI's unsuccessful one. Even clearer, and much more real, is the antagonism between the PCI and the Radical party. Behind the public statements and insincerely conciliatory tactics of the leader of the latter party since the elections, and behind the endless repertory of calls for unity directed to it by certain Communist spokesmen, the unprecedented asperity of the electoral clash between the two parties and the content of their mutual accusations reveal the real measure of their antagonism and their basic incompatibility. Each is quite right from its own standpoint: the PCI to doubt that the Radicals can in any way fit into the class Left as it understands it and at the same time to treat it as its most dangerous competitor; the Radicals to point to the affinity between the methods inspired by Marxist-Leninist totalitarianism and those of Fascism. In fact, because of the differences in their cultural backgrounds, in their way of approaching society, their internal organizations, their political behaviour, and the social, ethical and political models on which each of them are based, the two parties are divided by irreconcilable incompatibilities which are bound to grow sharper insofar as the Radicals are definitely aiming not just to deprive the PCI of the new electoral support it gathered in the 1970s but especially to confute, demystify and demolish its entire strategy.

Lastly, there is the Italian Socialist party (PSI). The fact that it gained a distinct if limited success in the European election of an extra 1.4 per cent compared with 1976, against a much greater gain made at the same time by the Social Democratic party (PSDI), which many observers had written off, show that in Italy as elsewhere socialist proposals and programmes have begun to appeal more to voters, for they feel they can trust the Socialists' attachment to the principles and institutions of liberal democracies. It may indeed be said that, even in the context of uncertainty about the real measure of the internal renewal of the PSI's parliamentary group and local leaders, the mere association of the party with the big social democratic parties in the European Parliament, and its new international links (which contrast completely with its perspectives of only a few years ago) provide a certain objective guarantee of its independence of the PCI, and perhaps even of some disagreement about political objectives. One may conclude that never before has the Italian Left appeared to have overcome so completely its inferiority complex in relation to the PCI, to be so little inclined to follow it uncritically nor to be so determined to challenge the PCI's hegemony and to set about wresting leadership from it. It is, of course, an open question whether this new resolve will succeed in finding ways to affect the realities of politics.

The situation which the elections have created outside the Left is now much less propitious compared to that prevailing hitherto. Since 1972 the PCI has been attempting to reach power not by putting itself forward as a normal democratic alternative to the party in power but rather by first undermining the latter and then ganging up with it as the guarantor and legitimizer of power itself. This is not just due to the relatively substantial increase in the strength of those intermediate parties such as the Liberals and Social Democrats which have most consistently opposed the prospect and the reality of the 'historic compromise' or the special relationship between the PCI and the DC; nor to the undoubted punishment of the Radical party which lost substantial votes in the European election. It is also due, however paradoxical it may seem, to the relative failure of the DC itself.

In the Italian general election the latter party gained no ground and in the European election it fell back considerably compared with 1976. Analysis of the regional figures, however, shows that in all northern and central regions except Lazio, it lost even more ground compared with 1976, which was considerable in the general election and often disastrous in the European. This reveals a basic fact. The premise on which it based its campaign (i.e. that the only real obstacle to the demands of the Communists and to the 'historic compromise' was a strengthened DC) was critically contrasted by a decisive part of the conservative electorate to all the policies and actions which in the preceding three years had in various ways helped to advance the PCI's claims and facilitated its approach to power, or had to some extent given it more weight in decision-making at every level. In simple terms, a decisive part of the electorate concerned took the view that a stronger DC would be a DC more inclined to continue, with still greater cynicism, its traditional power games and its long-standing trend towards a compromise with the PCI. The most mobile part of the conservative electorate, like its equivalent on the Left, saw the best guarantee against the convergence of the two major parties as lying outside these parties. For example, the various intermediate forces should break with, rather than reinforce, the logic of a two-party system. This fact is a confirmation of a still vigorous and indeed an increasing backlash in Italian society against the trends towards political colonization by the two big parties. The results of the referendum on the public financing of political parties had provided the first evidence of this backlash. This is a sign that the obstacles to the PCI's strategy have grown rather than diminished since 1977 and a markedly crucial phase has begun in its efforts to extend its influence on Italian society. What remains to be seen, of course, is whether the other parties will succeed in taking advantage of it.

Four months after the elections it became clear that the defeat inflicted on the PCI by the Italian people had not been translated either into an effective political opposition to its strategy by the other parties; nor into a corresponding reduction in its ability to block, veto, interfere with and distort the government's decision-making processes and activity; nor in any move to overcome the conditions of internal incoherence and powerlessness in which the Italian political system has been bogged down for a decade; nor in any consistent line pursued by the DC, the key party in the system. In the meantime we can see how the PCI has responded to its defeat. The explanation given is that it is due to the catastrophic historical and political situation of the Western world, of Europe and of Italy. The PCI insists that capitalist civilization and its internal and external relations are going through a crisis, giving rise to the inherent danger of authoritarian reaction and of threats to, or open attack upon, the historic conquests of the labour and socialist movement. Especially in Italy this danger might even lead to a coup d'état and this in itself makes more urgent and valid than ever the PCI's well-known proposal for an historic compromise – a joint government of all the main parties and the rejection of normal parliamentary alternations of power. Since the aim of such a joint government has to be the setting in motion of a substantial transformation of economic and social relations in the direction of socialism, the PCI intends to hasten its formation and, when it is formed, to move it in the appointed direction by arousing and leading great popular mass campaigns to demand such a transformation and crush the resistance of those who oppose it.

Meanwhile, during the summer since the 1979 elections, the party has completed its own internal reorganization which had been held over from its April conference. The new leadership of the PCI has been co-opted without exception from above, using the methods of the most rigid democratic centralism. It rigorously excluded anyone who, in the course of the conference debates, had put forward views capable of introducing real or potential alternatives in the decision-making process. As for the party structure, PCI General Secretary Berlinguer restated at the same session of the Central Committee of 3-7 July 1979 the total rejection of any move towards the adoption of an organizational model of the type employed by Western social democratic parties, for example votes on party policies and independence of parliamentary groups. Culturally and ideologically, according to its new constitution, the PCI continues to draw its inspiration from the Marxist, Leninist and Gramscian tradition of thought. Finally, when he met Brezhnev early in September 1979, Berlinguer made his own formal endorsement of the Soviet interpretation of the international situation: 'the successes of the Soviet people constitute an important contribution to the anti-imperialist and peace-loving forces throughout the world'; 'it is necessary to oppose decisively the campaigns of slander against the socialist countries and the movements of national liberation', and so on.

In relation to its organization, ideology, basic domestic and foreign strategy, leadership methods and composition, the PCI has thus quite unequivocally and brusquely reasserted and consolidated its most traditional and militant Leninist and Gramscian conceptions. In fact Berlinguer has said quite openly, in reply to sympathetic and non-hostile critics, that in a Communist party such matters as organization and leadership neither can, nor should be, modified and adjusted in the light of electoral failure. Even the observers who are most sympathetic to the PCI are thus constrained to acknowledge that the process of rethinking which they used to discern in the PCI has gone into reverse. One could conclude that the decision to 'dig in' intransigently on Leninist positions, if due to an attempt to regain control and placate the internal discontents of the party and fully reassert its traditional methods of relating to the masses, would nevertheless be paid for by the PCI in the form of a penalty. This could be a temporary reduction in its external credibility, and its ability to mobilize around it a certain understanding and deference, and, more concretely, to influence profoundly the political debate and balance within and between other parties and in the country generally. The fact that this has not occurred, and that the PCI has been able to entrench itself and re-Leninize itself, without paying a heavy price to compensate for it, is perhaps the most startling indication of the quality and extent of the crisis in Italian politics.

The means which have enabled the PCI to achieve this result can all be found in an article which Berlinguer published in 1979 before going on holiday to the Crimea, as a sort of message addressed to the rest of the Italian political class, especially to the DC, and more generally over the head of the latter to the whole establishment which in one way or another supports it. The basic concept in this article is that the decline of the country, the irreversible sharpening of the internecine struggle between the conflicting and sectional needs and demands of the different social groups, can only be avoided by creating a new political synthesis. This synthesis requires an alliance between forces which, whatever their differences, are in various ways prepared to support a truly revolutionary process, namely to impose structural transformations on the capitalist economy while at the same time spelling out how much they are prepared to yield in order to ensure the consent or at least the neutrality of other component forces of society. There must therefore be a compromise 'between those solely concerned with the level of production and those concerned with the content and quality of production'. The Secretary of the PCI does not give any hint of how these changes are to be brought about. But it is quite clear in the terms of the definition that what is mainly required is 'a new economic policy' carried out by the action of the working class in the shape of the PCI, 'not merely in relation to the distribution of wealth . . . but also on the form and quality of what is consumed and on the very process of accumulation'. The means employed are to be the abandonment of the 'old and unreliable mechanisms' of the market economy and the adoption of new methods which will 'permit the working class to achieve independent direct control, at least partially, of the use of resources'. Berlinguer shrugs off the problem of democratic centralism, accusing its critics of 'attacking parties as such', of wanting to 'combat and cut down to size all parties which tend to organize the masses and change society in the light of given ideals'. He also invites the DC to consider the proposition that 'its role and perhaps its very existence is at stake'. The article makes no reference to international problems.

Through this article the Secretary of the PCI was sketching out two interchangeable strategies. Firstly, that of an effective unity of the Left, mainly with the PSI. This would serve to block any steps taken independently by other parties on the Left which would leave the PCI in isolation and force it into positions it did not want to take up. Secondly, and more importantly, to cooperate and compromise, to discuss and agree with the DC. The first strategy had a very cold reception from the PSI, Radicals and Social Democrats, but the Catholics and the DC dignified the article as the basic gospel of Italian political debate, as if the future of the country depended on its assessment and interpretation and the answers to it. A few days later the closest collaborator of the Secretary of the DC deemed it 'a subject on which the forces of democracy can have fruitful encounters'. Others expressed their delight at 'the renewed attention' paid by the PCI to the Catholic world. At a subsequent seminar held by left-wing Catholics and Christian Democrats at Vallombrosa on 30 August-2 September 1979 Berlinguer's article was deferentially taken as the best starting-point for discussion by those who rejected the capitalist model, wished to prevent 'the alignment of the DC with the lay conservative parties of Europe' and proposed 'a different kind of development of the system', on the grounds that the capitalist and liberal-democratic model is flawed by tensions and injustices intolerable to Catholics. Finally, at the September meeting of the DC's National Executive the Secretary, while displaying the greatest hostility to the Socialists, acknowledged that the recent statements of the PCI had the merit of 'leaving room for a dialogue which he hoped would become deeper and more fruitful'.

Moreover, Catholic appreciation was not confined to these remarks, but extended to the *PCI's place in history* and to its whole function within the Italian political system. Leading Christian Democrats, including a former minister, publicly regretted the losses suffered by the PCI in the elections and regarded them as a destabilizing factor which endangered the balance of power on which democracy in Italy rests. In the struggle which then ensued as to the future policy of the DC and the composition of its leadership, this current of thought was expressed in the clearest terms. It maintained that the PCI should be recognized as the only true and legitimate representative of socialist traditions, aspirations and plans in Italy; as such it had to be regarded as one of the main props of Italian democracy. To debate with it and in some way to come to terms with it were not merely necessary but actually of help in ruling Italy and rescuing it from the crisis in which it is floundering. Such a debate and such a deal should therefore be the guiding principle of DC strategy. Since these views were merely a more vivid reflection of the basic attitude of the party's secretariat, in autumn 1979 the DC found itself responsible for having created a paradoxical situation. By taking as the main subject for its own internal debate a series of ideological propositions handed down to it by the PCI, it appeared unable to produce or even to assimilate any serious theoretical discussion of all the real and vital problems facing the country, for example the energy crisis, inflation, national defence, the obstacles to international economic cooperation, the crisis of the public services, and the worsening dualisms and inequalities of development. In order to improve its own internal relations and to hold open the door to any possible secret deal with the PCI (a party badly defeated in the elections, which had then been its main opponent and was now in opposition) it jeopardized its relations with the parties which supported a government led by a Christian Democrat and on which that government's duration and efficiency depended. In order to take temporary advantage of the readiness for compromise still flaunted by the PCI, the DC refrains from attacking the Leninist, totalitarian and pro-Soviet hard line which the latter is now pursuing in all directions. These paradoxes are too serious not to be the sign of profound distortions of the Italian political system.

My intention, in dwelling upon the description of these paradoxes and of the attitudes still prevailing in the DC, has simply been to exemplify and analyse the facts as a historian, rather than to employ the abstract definitions of political science or sociology, and so provide an adequate impression of how and to what extent the mechanisms of this system are today capable of evading, manipulating, falsifying and even reversing the impulses and the demands thrown up by the dynamic processes and deeper evolution of civil society. These dynamic processes, within crucial sectors of Italian society, have given rise to a clear rejection of the PCI's approach to politics and to an unprecedented defeat of its strategy. However, the political system, by its fragmentation and internal bickering, is once again restoring validity to this approach and strategy, and giving back to it enormous power to influence the relations between the other parties, all decision-making processes, the harmony of coalitions, the goals of legislation, the stability and duration of governments.

The main agent of this metamorphosis today is the crisis of the massive system of state control of the economy created in Italy and of the power system and consensus-forming mechanism which has made use of it, has battened upon it, and which is basically a tool of the DC. The faction of the Christian Democratic party which most fears that this crisis will catch up with it and sweep it away is precisely the section which sees in the PCI its most valid interlocutor and partner in the task of propping up that system and perhaps even strengthening it. Speeches about the need to preserve the popular soul of the DC, to correct the flaws and distortions of capitalism, to reject the liberal-democratic model, mean exactly what they say; and the rest is ideological metaphysics. From this point of view it appears to be perilous to dismantle state control, patronage and jobbery, to unshackle private enterprise, and to return to free collective bargaining. But to give more scope to the Leninist, Gramscian, democratic centralist, pro-Soviet PCI in the control of the vital organs of the economy, the administration and culture is acceptable.

This is not the place to describe and analyse state intervention in the Italian economy. However, some of its characteristics ought to be briefly mentioned here. First, those organizations and smaller companies which face extinction by not being able to finance themselves have come to depend on the brokerage of financial institutions for their very survival. However, these same financial institutions have now fallen under the direct or indirect control of politicians and are being administered according to criteria and goals which are mainly unrelated to business. Second, the public administration, which is government in all its forms, absorbs an ever-increasing proportion of national resources. But it does not use these to increase productive investments or to improve the efficiency of the social services, but rather to nourish and augment a jungle of overlapping bureaucracies in order to increase their powers and scope for action in relation to the economy, and bring about huge transfers of income on behalf of vested interests. Third, an abnormal number of goods and services benefit from generalized and untouchable subsidized prices which have never been part of any coherent plan, but which are useful for extending patronage to various interest groups. This system has now got to the point where the only way to maintain it is to allow an unhindered decline in accumulation, uncontrollable inflation at far higher levels than those of other industrial democracies, and tremendous damage to savings, just when international challenges make it urgent for the Italian economy to enjoy the maximum flexibility and undergo radical restructuring.

The processes outlined, although they have much in common with the crisis of the welfare state in all the industrial democracies, are quite obviously very different in many other respects. Their extent and seriousness depend in fact on the singular nature of the factors which gave rise to them and keep them going. There is no question that one of these factors is the presence of the strongest communist party operating in a free country. The revisionist image of itself which it has succeeded in creating in recent years should not lead us to forget that it still proposes to abolish the market economy and to install an economy which, if not completely state-owned, will certainly be directed entirely and compulsorily from the centre. The fact that the PCI is not a small sectarian and non-influential minority group but a large mass party intimately rooted in almost all social classes explains why this plan has been able to exert a deep influence on the real evolution of the Italian economy. All the forms of the class struggle which have occurred in Italy over the last twelve years have ultimately worked, consciously or not, to bring this plan to fruition. Even the activities of the trade unions have in the long term proved to be strictly in line with the Communist strategy.

In order to understand this connection one must realize that all the processes described earlier have been the direct result of some struggle or other by the unions and of the tremendous pressure they are able to exert. The unions have frozen all mobility in the factors of production in relation to the organization of labour, whether socially or at company level. They have imposed totally uneconomic hirings of staff in various branches of the public sector, have fiercely defended situations which were leading companies to disaster, have enforced the adoption of bureaucratic and welfare criteria in place of management criteria in the running of vast sectors of the national economy, have encouraged incorrect management decisions, and have stimulated unwise growth in public expenditure, etc.

Pressure from the PCI alone does not suffice to explain the spread of state interventionism in Italy unless account is also taken of one other factor, the internal degeneration of the Christian Democrats, still the largest political party and the governing party, which even during the last decade of crisis never stopped concentrating in its own grasp almost all the levers of state power. Its degeneration may be summarized as follows: the DC itself finally came to regard the extension of the public sector of the economy and the increasing interference of the state in the latter as an essential means of justifying its own proclaimed 'centrality' and 'irreplaceability' in the Italian political system and of keeping its control over the far-reaching processes of social change which were undermining the traditional bases of its power. Consequently it has never really opposed the trends I have just mentioned. It has always sought to turn them to its own temporary advantage and has often gone so far as to encourage them without openly admitting it.

One of the paradoxes of recent Italian history is that the laws which have given rise to many of the phenomena described have in practice been made by the rank and file of MPs, and are based on convergences between the DC and PCI which are no less real for being carefully disguised. By passing particular measures the DC believed it could avail itself of a new means for creating consensus and patronage. The PCI demanded or supported these measures because it correctly saw them as providing the essential basis for political and bureaucratic control. The PCI could see that these measures were laying the foundations for a system fundamentally in conformity with its own ideological vocation and its concept of the economy. The PCI knows that even if the system is temporarily controlled by others, one day it will itself gain control. Therefore it is not really a paradox that the result of this convergence in favour of state control has been a greater degree of disharmony, anarchy and ungovernability throughout the Italian economy.

CHAPTER SIX

The Communist Party and the Union of the Left in France

PHILIP NATAS

During the 1950s the French Socialist party allied itself with the Centre and the Right against the Communists. In 1958 Guy Mollet, the Socialist leader, went to Colombey-les-deux-Eglises to request General de Gaulle to return to head the French government. In the ensuing administration the French Socialist party supported the Gaullist government, and some Socialist party members even held ministerial positions. The Communist party was the main force within the opposition and was entirely isolated from other political forces, especially from the Socialist party. Yet the principal Communist party objective was to put an end to this separation and to build an alliance with the Socialist party; and it took fourteen years to sign a common programme of government between the two parties and to establish the alliance known as the *Union of the Left*. On 27 June 1972 the common programme was signed and the alliance officially established.

Five years later, in the spring of 1977, a victory for the Union of the Left seemed highly probable, and to some observers absolutely certain. But in April 1977 the Communist party asked that the common programme be brought up to date, and the discussions that followed became increasingly bitter. On 22 September 1977 the Communist party took the responsibility of breaking the Union of the Left and the common programme of government was abandoned. This rupture, and the dispute between the two parties, led to the failure of the Left in the general election of March 1978.

Three questions arise. First, why did the Communist party break the Union when its victory was nearly certain? Second, was this rupture a permanent aspect of the political scene or was the Union to be revived before the presidential election of 1981? Third, why did the Socialists accept the alliance with the Communists, since most of them thought during the 1960s that such a union could not last?

To attempt to answer these questions it is necessary to look at the evolution of the Socialist party since 1958, the position of the Socialists and Communists in 1979, and the possible future of the French Left as a whole.

The Evolution of the Socialist Party since 1958

Between 1958 and 1962 the policy of Guy Mollet, the French Socialist leader, diverged more and more from the policy of General de Gaulle. Guy Mollet, who had opposed the American government during the Suez crisis of 1956, was now accused of being an unconditional follower of the United States. During this period the Socialist party joined in the opposition to General de Gaulle. The Socialists were then labelled 'Atlanticists' by both the Gaullists and the Communists.

The Socialists, in the early years of the Fifth Republic, were also accused of being 'electoralists', meaning that they contracted alliances solely for purposes of electoral victory rather than on the basis of principle. In 1958 there were ten Communist representatives elected to the French Parliament, and few Socialists compared to the number of electoral votes in the country. It is important to understand that the electoral law was changed in 1958, making it difficult, and in many cases impossible, for the Left to elect representatives whilst the Socialists and Communists opposed each other. Consequently, in 1962 some Socialists were elected with the support of the Communists, who withdrew their own candidates. One of the Socialists elected was the leader, Guy Mollet.

After their break with de Gaulle, the Socialists had only two ways to get their representatives elected to the French Parliament. They could contract an alliance with either the Centrists or the Communists.

In 1964 Gaston Deferre, the Socialist mayor of Marseilles, became a presidential candidate in the 1965 election. After receiving the endorsement of the Socialist party he demanded one condition for maintaining his candidacy, the creation of a large federation comprising the centrist Christian party (MRP), the centre-left Radical party and his own Socialist party. Guy Mollet, who opposed this federation, of which he would not have been the leader, helped disrupt the negotiations for its establishment. Gaston Deferre withdrew his candidacy and Guy Mollet was then free to build a new federation – Fédération de la Gauche Démocrate et Socialiste (FGDS) – which comprised the Centre-Left Radical party, the Socialist party and François Mitterrand's small party, the Convention des Institutions Républicaines (CIR). Because the Centrist MRP was not part of this movement, it became known as the 'small federation'. With the assistance of Guy Mollet, François Mitterrand became the first President of the FGDS. He was endorsed by the new Federation *and* the Communist party as candidate for President of the French Republic.

For the first round of the election on 5 December 1965

Mitterrand, as candidate of the Left, received 31.7 per cent of the votes, but for the final round when he was the candidate of all the Republicans, including many anti-Gaullists from the Right, he won 44.8 per cent of the votes. Gaston Deferre, leader of the most moderate wing of the party, supported Mitterrand but, like Guy Mollet, he too was opposed to the common programme requested by the Communist party.

After de Gaulle's re-election Gaston Deferre tried to recapture the leadership of the Socialist party through a reformist platform and was opposed to a close union with the Communist party.

In 1967 the de Gaulle-Giscard d'Estaing coalition won a one-vote majority in the National Assembly. The Centrists of Jean Lecanuet were in opposition to the government and the majority but without ties to the Left in the National Assembly. Most of the Socialist representatives were elected with the support of the Communist party in the final round of the election. At this time the coalition between the non-communist Left and the Communist party was only for electoral purposes. A common programme of government was rejected by the two wings of the Socialist Party, the dominant party of the FGDS. No Socialist-Communist government was expected even in the event of a victory to the Left, and there were no Communists at that time in the French shadow Cabinet.

In 1966 four bright young men joined the Socialist party and founded the Centre d'Etudes et de Recherches Socialistes (CERES). This Centre became the left wing of the party, supporting the common programme of government requested by the Communist party. Within the Socialist party it supported Guy Mollet against the more moderate Gaston Deferre.

In the parliamentary elections of 1968 de Gaulle won more than fifty per cent of the vote without the help of either Giscard's party or the Centrist party of Jean

Lecanuet. The Left was defeated and the subsequent conflict within the Socialist party led to the candidacy of Gaston Deferre, who received only five per cent in the following presidential election of 1969. Most of the Socialist voters in that election chose Alain Boher, the Centrist candidate. After that defeat of 1969 the CERES advocated the common programme of government with the Communist party more and more assertively.

In 1969 a contradictory situation appeared among the elected Socialists. Most of the representatives were elected with the Communists' support, but at the municipal level most of the Socialists elected in large cities were supported by the Centrists against the Communist party. The two wings of the party had at this time two coalition policies. The situation was further complicated by the fact that some of the Socialist mayors of the larger cities were generally elected against the Communist candidate, and at the national level representatives with Communist support were elected against their local allies. In 1969 many moderate Socialists set up a group called the Démocratie Socialiste (DS), which put out a publication advocating a reformist platform and opposing not only the common programme but even the electoral coalition with the Communist party as a permanent commitment.

In June 1971 there was a General Assembly, referred to as 'le Congrès d'Epinay', which marked the beginning of the new Socialist party. François Mitterrand joined the party with his followers, who were members of the CIR, and he was subsequently elected the leader of the new party. This meeting is now generally regarded as the beginning of a sharp move towards the common programme and the Union of the Left.

Actually the support of the moderates of the DS was essential to the election of François Mitterrand as head of the new Socialist party. The political situation at the time was ambiguous as presented by the news media. The only paper which detected the alliance between Francois Mitterrand and the moderates was *l'Humanité*, the Communist party daily, which viewed the alliance with the right wing of the Socialist party with some anxiety. At a meeting of the central committee of the Communist party, Georges Marchais, its General Secretary, reminded his comrades of his concern about the Congrès d'Epinay. Georges Marchais' suspicions about the Socialist party, and especially its new leader, François Mitterrand, were to remain a central feature determining PCF strategic thinking.

Between June 1971 and September 1977, although there were many fluctuations in detailed policy and in personnel, the Union of the Left and the common programme remained the settled policy of the Socialist party.

In 1973 the Union of the Left failed to win a majority in the National Assembly. In 1974 François Mitterrand lost the presidential election. In 1977 the strategy of the Union of the Left was applied at the municipal level and the Communist party doubled the number of its elected members. In the large cities everywhere alliances between Centrists and Socialists were broken and replaced by coalitions between Communists and Socialists. It was a success for the Union of the Left and consequently this same strategy was extended to all types of elections.

The Position of the French Left in the Early Eighties

Likely developments in the next few years, and in the short time left before the presidential contest in 1981, will depend upon the nature of evolution within the Socialist party, the trade unions, and within the Communist party; and upon developments between them. We should look at each in turn.

Since 1971 the Socialist party has completely rejected the Third Force Strategy, which was another term for the alliance with the Centrists. The Congrès d'Epinay resulted in a rupture with the previous kind of coalition and the old tradition of the French Socialist party (SFIO), which was essentially social democratic in practice. It also marked what was labelled as a strategy for a rupture in capitalism.

In 1972 the Socialist party published its own programme of government, a 240-page document which reflects the great changes in ideology which followed upon the change in strategy.

A new concept appears in this programme, that of 'irreversibility'. This concept is first mentioned in Francois Mitterrand's introduction, where he speaks of 'irreversible measures' and 'permanent acquisition'. It is then mentioned in Chapter 2, 'Immediate or Irreversible Measures'.

The new anti-capitalist strategy implies that the objective of the Socialist party is the socialization or collectivization of the main means of production and exchange. This collective ownership is supposed to take several forms, including direct state ownership or self-managed – that is worker-managed – companies. A minimum threshold of collectivization and nationalization is stated in the first part of the programme, entitled 'Economic Democracy'. It was also stated that if a company's workers request the collectivization of their company, the issue would be brought to Parliament so that the minimum threshold could be quickly extended.

In foreign policy the Socialist party remained in favour of the construction of a United Europe, but with many restrictions. The most important changes in foreign policy concerned relations with the Third World and the communist countries, and in February 1975 at the Pau convention the party voted for a motion reflecting these changes. It is said, for instance, that a truly amicable relationship has been created with Fidel Castro and that the party is in contact with most of the revolutionary movements in Latin America and Africa.

In May 1976 a Socialist party delegation went to Hungary at the invitation of the Hungarian Communist party, and a joint communiqué stated that the French Socialist delegation was favourably impressed by the successes achieved in the construction of socialism by the Hungarian people under the direction of the working class and its party.

It is fair to say that in some Socialist publications the socialist nature of the communist regimes is denied and in others implied.

If the Cuban regime is judged amicable, then the United States is often spoken of as 'imperialist', especially by the CERES group within the party.

Since the Metz meeting in 1979 the party has been managed by the Mitterrand group, who only received a plurality of the votes, and the CERES faction. The two less powerful factions, led by Michel Rocard and Pierre Mauroy respectively, who are regarded as social democratic by CERES, are opposed to this left-leaning new direction. In fact, Rocard's conception of socialism is more decentralized than that of the majority and argues that the market does not need to be completely destroyed, that it has a role to play in a socialist society. Michel Rocard often speaks of the necessity for the Socialist party to think rigorously and realistically on economic matters. But the fact remains that whatever the differences between the four groups, the Union of the Left and the rupture with capitalism continue to be the strategy and the goal of the party today. Few Socialists contemplate attempting to forge an alliance with the Centrist forces, even in the wake of the rupture between Socialists and Communists in 1977. On the contrary, even with an aggressive Communist party, each group thinks that in the future some form of new alliance has to be found.

The unions have political leanings in France. The CGT is well known as being Communist-dominated but three other union organizations have Socialist leaders, namely the CFDT, the FO and the FEN. The latter is the school and university teachers' union and is led by a Socialist, elected by a broad coalition opposed to Communist leadership. The CFDT is led by a majority close to Rocard's wing of the Socialist party, and the FO is a reformist union led by a Socialist who is clearly a social democrat opposed to the CGT, the Communist party and the Union of the Left. Even though the trade unions are an important feature of French political and industrial life, the future of the French Left is unlikely to be determined by the unions themselves. In any event, the unions, particularly the CGT, are not autonomous political animals; the Communist party, in effect, will determine the future of the French Left, the Union of the Left, and in all probability, the outcome of the 1981 elections.

Recent developments in the Communist party do not augur well for the establishment of any genuine alliance of left-wing forces. The Communist party appears to be set on a course that is increasingly narrow, sectarian and Moscow-oriented. Arguably, the first signs of this narrow approach appeared in 1977.

Why did the Communist party break the Union of the Left in September 1977? Only a few people in the Communist leadership know the complete answer to this question. Part of the answer can be found in the doctrine of Marxism-Leninism, which says that the Communist party is the party of the working class, which implies that it is the only one. The Communists never saw the Union of the Left as a union between two equal partners. As

François Mitterrand said for the Socialist party: 'The Communist party would have gladly accepted the victory of a Left alliance in which it would be the dominant party, electorally and ideologically, which means acceptance of the Communist proposals.'

This explanation certainly accounts for one main reason, but are there possibly other explanations? Lionel Jospin, the spokesman for the Socialist party, hypothesized that 'an explanation of an international nature' was a distinct possibility but that 'it was difficult to determine', adding that 'the will of the Soviets to maintain the political and social status quo in Europe was not contradictory to the Communist party's own reasons'. Again, this explanation seems plausible but it implies that some motives may exist that we do not yet know of. Anyway, it must be remembered that in September 1977 the Communist proposals in economic matters would have given management of most of the new nationalized industries to the Communist party. The Socialist party did not yield to these demands and the Union of the Left broke up on 22 September 1977.

All the signs are that as the eighties unfold Communist party intransigence is solidifying. The Communist party appears to have abandoned most of its previous 'Eurocommunist' pretences – it was never, of course, particularly comfortable in this role – and is reverting quite openly to a hard-line, neo-Stalinist, pro-Moscow position. The more 'liberal' opposition that arose within the Communist party, particularly amongst some of its intellectual supporters, following the 1978 election, has been firmly squashed. Furthermore, the PCF took the lead in organizing the international Communist party gathering of 1980, held in Paris, which Moscow insisted upon and the Italian and Spanish Communist parties were severely reticent about.

In the coming presidential election it is virtually certain

that there will be more than one candidate for the Left, namely Georges Marchais for the Communist party and François Mitterrand for the Socialist party.

Other candidates for the non-communist Left are possible, and M. Crepeau, leader of the Mouvement des Radicaux de Gauche, is already a candidate. That Georges Marchais could collect more votes than anybody else on the Left is a real possibility.

An opinion poll run by SOFRES l'Expansion in November 1979 showed that President Giscard d'Estaing would be the winner against Francois Mitterrand, Michel Rocard or Georges Marchais with 53, 52 and 66 per cent of the votes respectively. The presidential election is not until 1981 and much can happen before then to change the present outlook. In any case, the chances are that the Communist party will be in the race with its own candidate and that the campaign will be very different from the last one, especially the campaign of the Left.

The reversion of the PCF to a hard-line strategy, one nevertheless based upon what has always been its inherent Leninist character, has two consequences. First, it disproves many of the fanciful notions (very fashionable in liberal circles throughout the West in the mid-seventies) that even the French Communist party could be embraced within a generic conception of West European Communism known as 'Eurocommunism'. Independence from Moscow, a commitment to pluralism in the economy and to human rights politically, a more democratic internal party organization − none of these conceptions, the core ideas of the 'Eurocommunist' nation, can be attributed to the PCF as it develops in the early eighties.

Secondly, as the French Communist party becomes increasingly hostile to the democratic consensus and more obviously pliant to Moscow's demands, the outlook for French democratic Socialists looks bleak. The French Left will be divided, as the Socialists cannot possibly compromise with the PCF; but, without an agreement, the Socialists cannot win power at presidential level. Whether the French democratic Left will continue to *seek* an agreement with the PCF, will attempt a new 'centre-force' movement or will break up under the strains, cannot be prophesied.

CHAPTER SEVEN

The West German Social Democratic Party

PAUL FRIEDRICH

In 1949 the Federal Republic of Germany held the first elections for the Bundestag. The Social Democrats (SPD) were profoundly disappointed that the first Chancellor of the new post-war Republic was not to be drawn from their ranks. Many Social Democrats thought they were the rightful heirs to power following the defeat of Nazism; but such expectations were not to be satisfied by the electorate. Following a second defeat in 1953 the SPD set about attempting to clarify the party's aims and policies. Calls for reform came from various sections of the party. The 'Burgermeister group' (including Willy Brandt and Ernst Reuter in Berlin, Wilhelm Kaiser in Bremen and Max Bauer in Hamburg) argued for the development of practical policies of reform and administration; Heinrich Dienst developed an analysis of post-war economy based upon a practical application of Keynes and notions of the mixed economy; Erich Ollenhauer wanted to build the SPD as an efficient political machine which could compete electorally with the ascendant Christian Democracy of Konrad Adenauer.

The further electoral defeat of 1957, when the Christian Democrats (CDU) obtained more than half the votes, concentrated the mind of the SPD leadership and made an urgent political and intellectual reappraisal even more necessary. This reappraisal led to the adoption of the *Godesberg Programme*, named after the SPD conference held at Bad Godesberg in 1959. This 1959 conference overthrew the 'Marxist heritage' of the party; but in some respects it went even further. It boldly announced that democratic socialism 'declares no ultimate truths'. Even the role of planning and public ownership was played down – certainly more so than was the case in many other left-of-centre West European parties. The Godesberg Programme declared in favour of 'as much competition as possible, as much planning as necessary'. The SPD also committed itself, roundly and proudly, to the parliamentary and democratic system: the aim of the party was to 'gain the confidence of the majority of the people in . . . an equal competition with the other democratic parties'. At the same time the SPD reaffirmed its resolute support for the Western alliance system.

In many respects the Godesberg Programme set the SPD on a course which could not even properly be described as 'socialist'. The SPD had, in effect, become a 'social democratic' party; and was developing an approach to politics which was to become the model for social democrats throughout the Western world. When I myself became a member of the SPD it was to support its post-Godesberg orientation, and even the term 'democratic socialism' had disappeared for all practical purposes. A small socialist minority, some of them drawing on the neo-Marxist ideas of Wolfgang Abendroth and other intellectuals who resisted the revisionism of the fifties, left the SPD after Godesberg. They set out to create socialist organizations, particularly in the universities.

Yet the notion of 'democratic socialism' (as opposed to 'social democracy') was to have a renaissance in the late 1960s. The student movement of the mid-sixties and the entry of the SPD into the 'Grand Coalition' between 1966 and 1969 resurrected a 'left wing' within the SPD which, although never in the ascendant, opened the door for years of ideological debate about the true nature of the Godesberg Programme. 'Social democracy' versus 'democratic socialism', a seemingly semantic exercise, nevertheless became the banners under which our increasingly fierce battle within the party in the late sixties and early seventies was conducted.

Behind all of this stood a search for identity, the claim to represent the right interpretation, something we call *Selbstverständnis* in German. The SPD during this period became a broad coalition of heterogeneous forces. Under different circumstances, particularly under different election laws, the feuding within the SPD might have caused splits: indeed the party might easily have broken up into several parties, ranging from a socialist Left party at one end to a reformist Centre party at the other.

Broadly speaking the SPD 'Left' of the early 1970s can best be defined in terms of policy. On the political level the SPD 'Left' consistently rejected coalitions or alliances with the Christian Democrats. However, ever since 1969 when the SPD entered into a coalition with the Free Democrats (when Willy Brandt became Chancellor) the SPD leadership has not needed to fight on this front. On foreign and defence issues the SPD 'Left' tended to oppose West German membership of NATO, West German support for the American involvement in Vietnam, and the emergency legislation plans of the government in Bonn. Also, the 'Left' were in the forefront of developing the new policies, which began under the Brandt Chancellorship, towards Eastern Europe and the German Democratic Republic; even so, the 'Ostpolitik' did secure a wide consensus of support within the SPD ranging from enthusiastic to cautious. The 'Left' also wanted the SPD/FDP administration to spend more of West Germany's resources upon aid to the Third World.

Other, domestic, rallying issues for the 'Left' included:

greater concentration upon urban problems, rent control, real estate profit control, radical redistributive tax reforms, easing of conscientious objection limitations for service in the armed forces, and better conditions for immigrant workers (*Gastarbeiter*). There was also a concentrated campaign for new structures and organizational reforms within the universities, which was not surprising bearing in mind that many of the left-wing activists of the period came into the SPD from out of the radicalized university sector.

During this period, and into the seventies, the 'Jusos' of the SPD (the party's youth wing) received considerable publicity and appeared to many to be a very real political force, one that was certainly contained by the leadership but one that would take over the party, and move it in a leftward direction, at a later stage. Certainly the 'Jusos' themselves continued to portray themselves as a force to be reckoned with and as 'the SPD of the eighties'. Yet this prediction has certainly not materialized; and is unlikely to.

For anyone with a feel for the politics of the SPD, and for the political and economic realities with which it has to live, it is obvious that the bid for power by the left wing of the SPD, led by the 'Jusos', was a failure. The SPD Left was, essentially, defeated at the party congress in Hanover in April 1973; and has been effectively contained ever since. In a sense, the conflict within the SPD was resolved when Helmut Schmidt took office as Chancellor in May 1974. Schmidt represents the orthodox social democratic wing of the party; and his political pedigree is certainly more to the right than that of his predecessor, Willy Brandt. Schmidt is a dedicated supporter of the Western alliance, as his period as the Federal Republic's defence minister amply displayed; and his practical, problem-solving political nature makes him distrust and indeed abuse ideological predilections.

As it enters the eighties the SPD, as far as domestic politics are concerned, remains well within the social democratic consensus. It manages the most efficient mixed economy of all the major industrial nations of the West; its grip upon inflation, certainly by comparison with its major competitors, is relatively firm; industrial relations are relatively tranquil. The SPD leadership continues to see itself as developing policies which will give it the means of conducting, governing and managing the country's affairs in an efficient, rather than an ideological, manner.

On the SPD Left there has been something of a change. No longer is the leadership of the party confronted by a radical student generation; there appears to be a political disengagement from the problems of the sixties — more because of a lack of motivation than because many of the problems have been solved. To a large extent this is the result of what some commentators have described as the 'occupational therapy' which the youth of the sixties have recently undergone. Also, the experience of the Brandt Chancellorship — particularly its Ostpolitik — took some of the wind out of the sails of the 'progressive Left' within the party. Yet new issues have arisen to take the place of the old sixties issues as the rallying point for 'Left and progressive' members of the SPD. First, there is a keen opposition to the *Berufsverbot*, the constitutional law governing entry into the public service; 'the Left' opposes government policy which requires that extremists should not be allowed to serve the state. Secondly, there is opposition to the new anti-terrorist legislation. Thirdly, and most significantly, there is the ecological issue. This centres upon the debate about the role which nuclear energy should play within the West German economy, a debate made more crucial following the rise in oil prices, the lack of certainty in oil supply and the dependence of the West German economy on oil from politically unstable areas of the world.

These new issues which divide 'Left' from 'Right' within the SPD are in one sense only partly 'new'. Within them we can see the contours of the previous identity crisis which afflicted the SPD. Certainly the old 'socialist' versus 'social democratic' debate is still present and today's divisions reflect basic instincts about whether or not the party wants to make the social market economy work. It remains, in part, a battle between those who want to transform the system and those who do not. At the heart of the present divisions, and they are only marginally Left/Right in traditional terms, is the question of morality versus efficiency. On the one hand there is the governing faction, led and symbolized by Helmut Schmidt, which views the SPD as an efficient means of governing and managing a complex society. On the other hand there are those who long for a party which can assert moral goals and values. The split is not, at least primarily, between Helmut Schmidt and the left wing; the problem is rather the alienation of part of the membership of the SPD from a party which they no longer believe gives them *moral guidance*.

This search for moral guidance appears to be the main preoccupation of the post-student revolt generation. This generation are politically demobilized even though many of them are still, formally at least, members and supporters of the SPD. It is amongst this alienated group that the ecologists find their potential voters and supporters. The ecologist movement could have serious consequences for the future electoral politics of the Federal Republic and particularly for the SPD. If the ecologists succeed in drawing votes away from the SPD but at the same time cannot achieve the necessary five per cent of the national vote to secure parliamentary representation, then CDU/CSU government becomes a distinct possibility. Apart from any other considerations the ecology question poses a serious dilemma for the SPD leadership: if it maintains its moderate, rational and efficient programme and leadership it risks going into opposition; if it makes compromises with the ecology movement, and indeed with the 'politics of morality' generally, it may lose much of its traditional urban and suburban affluent worker support.

Yet the future of the SPD, and of the factions within the SPD, may depend more upon foreign and defence questions than even upon the developing schisms over domestic policy. The SPD, particularly Brandt, Wehner and Bahr, was the architect of the Ostpolitik. The attempt to improve relations with the GDR and to lower tensions between West and East in central Europe is seen by the SPD leadership as being in the 'national interest' of the Federal Republic. It is also a popular policy with the general public, as it has eased somewhat the previously rigid divisions which precluded family reunions across the borders of West and East Germany. For these reasons, as well as the desire to avoid another crisis over Berlin, the SPD leadership has persisted with détente, a geopolitical strategy which has come under increasing criticism in many other Western nations.

At the same time the SPD leadership has given firm support to NATO. There has never been any question of its loyalty to the aims and principles of the Atlantic alliance. Chancellor Schmidt publicly supported the programme for the neutron bomb before the concept was abandoned by President Carter. The West German government has also accepted the NATO proposal to station Cruise missiles on its territory and a motion to that effect was carried through the 1979 party congress of the SPD by the leadership with a hefty majority. The Federal Republic has also taken the lead in bolstering the economy of the key NATO nation of Turkey. Neither the 'special relationship' with Paris nor the commitment to détente can be seen, in the ultimate, as irreconcilable with West German NATO commitments.

The SPD leadership sees no irreconcilability between the

pursuit of legitimate and different national interests amongst the members of the alliance and the obligations of the Atlantic alliance. The problem for the SPD, and indeed for the CDU/CSU will come if the world situation, essentially the East/West conflict, significantly worsens in the coming years. A lot will depend upon how West German public opinion reacts to a worsening East/West, USA/USSR situation.

If détente with the East is permanently abandoned by the major Western power, and if a consensus builds up within the Federal Republic behind such an abandonment, then the SPD is likely to be more seriously divided than the CDU/CSU. There still remains a corpus of opinion within the SPD that supports disarmament measures and seeks an even deeper relaxation of tensions between the two Germanys; and in a new international atmosphere an opposition faction, based upon the post-student generation, could cause the SPD leadership some problems.

Even so, and no matter what the changing international situation, the SPD will continue to pursue the general lines of policy that have characterized the party since the Godesberg programme, certainly so if the party retains power in Bonn. If the party should go into opposition the tensions within it would naturally increase, but even then they are probably containable.

CHAPTER EIGHT

Trends in the Scandinavian Left

DAVID GRESS

Historical Background

Left-wing politics in Scandinavia are predominantly social democratic politics. Large working-class parties, based on the revolutionary ideology of the German socialists, arose in the last third of the nineteenth century. In Denmark and Sweden they called themselves Social Democratic parties; in Norway the party is called the Labour party. In all cases they obtained their votes from the urban working class which developed during the industrialization of Scandinavia, a process which began around 1860 and was basically not completed until after the Second World War (at which time more than half of the GNP of the Scandinavian countries came from trade and industry, not agriculture).

The orientation and doctrines of these parties closely paralleled that of the German Social Democratic party, and this connection has to some extent persisted until today. What this basically means is that the ideology of the working-class political party was not native to Scandinavia and had no local roots such as British socialism had, for example, in certain aspects of religious nonconformism and utopian beliefs. Scandinavian working-class parties were precisely that — parties fighting for a transformation of society in the interests of the industrial proletariat and at the expense of the existing order, both that of the industrial owners and the large landowners, *and* also of the 'radical' tradition of liberalism which was particularly strong in Denmark (being descended in part from the existentialism of Kierkegaard).

These parties, then, saw themselves as exceptional, not part of the usual political spectrum. There were debates, as in the French and German parties, between the revolutionary and the reformist wings, but both agreed that they were 'not like the others'. The foreign nature of their doctrines helped to preserve this 'exceptionalism' and prevented the formation of a common front with, for example, the farmers' party in Denmark (called Venstre, the 'Left' party, in opposition to the Right, the party of the large landowners), even though this party was fighting for the principle of government by the majority in Parliament and for other democratic aims.

After 1917, communist parties were formed in all the Scandinavian countries. This very soon had the effect, as it did in Germany, of 'normalizing' the large parties, the social democrat parties. In the twenties they abandoned their revolutionary claims, and around 1930 they came to power on their own in all three of the major Scandinavian countries — Denmark, Sweden and Norway. Since then, they have been absolutely dominant (they governed in Sweden without interruption from 1932 to 1976, and in Denmark from 1929 to 1942 and from 1947 until now with only six years out of office). This has meant that political debate and public discussion has largely been carried out on the basis of social democratic policies. These parties dictated the terms of debate and to a large extent carried out the debate as well, to the point that not even the conservative party in Sweden (called the Moderate Union party) dares to attack the welfare state and its bureaucracy for fear of being denounced as antisocial, inhuman and reactionary.

But the parties were still exceptional in that they still did not see themselves and were not seen as 'normal' parties. This has only begun to change in the last twenty years. The problem I want to address in this chapter, then, has two aspects: what has been the content of social democratic policy and debate — the terms on which future planning has taken place in all the Scandinavian countries — and to what extent have the social democratic parties actually accepted the principles of the democratic system, of the possibility of changing governments and changing social and political aims in society? To put it differently, in terms of a highly fruitful approach to the study of politics and international relations: is the 'political culture' of the social democratic parties of Scandinavia still recognizably different from that of the parties of the Centre and Right, referred to in Scandinavia as the 'bourgeois' parties? If not, how does the political culture of social democracy differ, and what does this portend for the future of the democratic system in Scandinavia and for the West as a whole? Finally, if there indeed has been a process of assimilation, of absorption of the working-class parties by the surrounding 'capitalist' culture, is this process still continuing, has it stopped, or has it gone into reverse? These are all questions which are rarely addressed in Scandinavia itself, where the debate usually turns on very narrow and immediate issues (economic policy), and my answers to them are therefore in large part impressionistic and provisional.

I shall have some words to say later about other left-wing groups (in the traditional and still useful sense of groups that derive their doctrines and vocabulary from some form of Marxism or socialism), both within and without the formal structures of the social democratic parties. At this point I merely repeat that, as I said at the outset, the Scandinavian Left is very largely social democratic. The communist parties have never (except in Finland) constituted more than a minute fraction of the population. Just after the Second World War they scored some gains in Denmark and Norway, as a result of the widespread feeling that the Soviet Union had borne the brunt of the war effort and the even more widespread wilful or ideological ignorance of the nature of the Stalinist regime. But these gains evaporated as soon as normality and economic activity had been restored. In the last ten years, the CPs have attempted to use the crisis, or rather the sense of crisis which they themselves assiduously try to foster, to regurgitate doctrines proclaiming the imminent demise of 'state monopoly capitalism' and so forth. There is no doubt that many workers were, and are, dissatisfied with the posture of the social democratic parties, and the CPs did recover some of what they had lost in the fifties and sixties. There are now signs, however, that these renewed gains will prove even more ephemeral than those of the immediate post-war period. The Danish CP has just lost its parliamentary representation; the Swedish CP is now Eurocommunist, having broken with Moscow, and retains a foothold in the Riksdag (its seats have always been used by the Social Democratic party to secure its majority, but with no noticeable effect on social democratic policy as such); and in Norway the CP has been completely undercut by a vigorous effort on behalf of the Labour party to win radical votes and prevent them from going to the Communists. Finland, of course, is a special case, as it is forced to deal with the Soviet Union in a manner and to a degree quite unlike that of any other ostensibly Western country; there are two CPs, one pro-Moscow and one nationalist, and the latter is now part of the governing coalition with the Social Democrats. There is no sign that the popular support of these parties is increasing.

There is therefore no immediate or plausible danger from the CPs as such. The danger comes rather from Communist penetration of important unions (in Denmark, the union of seamen, not affiliated to the LO (corresponding to the TUC), is largely Communist, but its secretary has just been expelled from the party) and from such things as Communist attempts to close *Berlingske Tidende*, Denmark's largest morning paper and the world's oldest continuously appearing daily. *Berlingske* has been threatened with closure for the past several years for the very simple reason that Communists in the print rooms sabotage the production and distribution of the paper literally every night (through absenteeism, sudden 'sick days', having meals at crucial times of production, forcing the paper to hire extra hands and airplanes to fly copies to distant distribution centres, etc.). There can be no doubt that this activity is a flagrant breach of contract, apart from infringing the paper's constitutional right to be published as an organ of free speech, but as clear-cut as the case is, it is impossible to prove, and the management of the paper is currently attempting to force manning reductions by promising to fire an equivalent number of freelance and other 'marginal' contributors on the one hand, and on the other by appealing to the vast majority of print workers who have no interest in seeing their place of work taken away. The matter is still very much up in the air.

To conclude this section: 'formal' communism and its explicit rejection of democratic procedures has never appealed to Scandinavians. What might give more rise to worry at the present time is the growing influence of 'loose' Marxism and unaffiliated, largely academic socialism which has infiltrated large parts of the social democratic movements apart from having formed parties of its own (in Denmark; in Sweden it is almost impossible

to create new political parties, as I shall describe below).
The characteristics of this academic socialism are familiar
enough in this country: a belief in corporatism and
collectivism, the rights of 'groups' and 'organizations'
over those of the 'individual', individualism conceived as
reactionary and selfish, contempt for the free market and
commercial relations, fear of freedom in the sense that
adherents of this academic socialism prefer positions as
civil servants in the media or at the universities and in the
schools and actively fight those who operate outside these
structures, and a considerable degree of naïveté and
misinformation on matters of global importance. This
body of opinion is growing and extending its influence
through the agencies and institutions of government,
education and information. It is to a discussion of these
opinions and their importance, and their relation to and
role in social democratic movements and policies as such
that I now turn.

Issues in Individual Countries

Denmark

The knowledge abroad of the political situation in
Denmark over the past five years or so can probably be
summed up in one word: Glistrup. The name of the leader
of the anti-tax 'Progress party' has become a catchword,
most famously for his announcement that, were he to
become prime minister, he would replace the armed forces
by a taped recording saying (in Russian): 'We surrender.'
His notoriety probably conceals the single most important
fact about him and his party: their total lack of influence
on Danish politics. One would have thought it impossible
for political life to go on as before after the election of
November 1973, in which Glistrup vaulted to prominence
in Parliament with twenty-eight seats, which made the
Progress party the second largest in the country. All the

other parties suffered losses, most disastrously the Conservatives, where Glistrup got much of his support. But nevertheless, faced with this declaration of no confidence in the old parties, a declaration by the voters which it would be fair to say was unprecedented in the history of Danish parliamentary democracy, those same old parties went on absolutely as before. The only noticeable change was, perhaps, some degree of overspending and extravagance intended to show that the old parties were *not* going to be frightened by Glistrup into retrenchment and cutbacks. Glistrup's impact can thus be said to have been almost wholly negative: it demonstrated serious communication and credibility gaps in the public life of the country, and it deprived any policy of restraint and retrenchment of any chance of success, because such policy became identified with Glistrup, and for obscure and not quite comprehensible reasons, none of the old parties felt able to distinguish between the (possibly unpleasant and dishonest) character of Mr Glistrup himself and the perfectly sensible criticisms he made of the overgrown welfare bureaucracy and expenditure.

Glistrup and his party were convient to the Left as well, in that they could use him as a bogey man and proof of the ineradicable stupidity and repressive character of the 'bourgeois' wing of Danish voters. Glistrup polarized politics in Denmark by challenging and exacerbating the strength of modish leftism and academic socialism. This coincided with economic difficulties so that all the bureaucrats, academics and media people who might normally have been apolitical or mildly social democratic became pushed to the left, either out of fear for their own position and the consequent demands for job security, expansion of the public sector and more guarantees of group and organization 'rights', or out of a genuine contempt for a population so many of whom could actually vote for Mogens Glistrup.

While the Glistrup phenomenon cannot, of course, excuse the fiscal irresponsibility and shortsightedness of the Social Democratic government formed in 1975 and again in 1979, it serves to explain it. It also serves to explain why the Liberal party (the old farmers' party, still curiously enough called 'Venstre', meaning the 'Left') government of November 1973-February 1975 failed to carry out a much-needed programme of economic belt-tightening and incomes policies. They were simply afraid of obstruction by the Social Democrats and the labour movement, because any such strict programme would be suspected of being influenced by 'Glistrup'.

The latest election, that of 23 October 1979, has for the first time since 1973 shown a marked shift back towards the five 'old' parties: the Social Democrats, the Centre party (which split from 'Venstre' in 1905), the Conservatives, the Liberals and the Socialist Peoples' party, which began as a breakaway group from the CP after the Hungarian uprising in 1956. The current position is a repetition of the classic pattern of the thirties, fifties and sixties: a Social Democratic minority government, based on the shifting support of the Centre party and (occasionally) of the Socialists.

The Glistrup phenomenon may, therefore, be receding. It also seems likely that Glistrup himself will be out of Parliament within a year, as he is fighting a public suit for massive tax evasion. But this does not and will not bring the situation back to the 'comfortable' pattern of the sixties. Not only are the immediate problems very serious indeed (it remains to be seen whether the Social Democratic government can, or will, deal with them), but the Social Democrats themselves have changed. The old guard of reformist Social Democrats, believing in improving life-chances for as many as possible, have been dying out. Their younger replacements are more ideological, more committed to organization, planning and regimentation and quite astonishingly unable to comprehend the basic principles and values of an open society. The 'political culture' of the Social Democrats is changing, but it is not simply changing back to the revolutionary, proletarian fervour of 1920 and earlier. It is changing toward a more theoretical, academically influenced stance which is actually quite distant from the aspirations of most voters. For example, a Social Democratic demand for some years now has been 'economic democracy', which basically means the gradual expropriation of industry into the hands of huge 'public' funds administered by the LO. Polls have shown that this idea commands minute support in the population. The election rhetoric during the latest campaign did avoid the term 'economic democracy', and spoke instead of 'compulsory profit-sharing' which implies a far less drastic intervention. But an intervention it remains, and it has been clearly stated by the LO leadership that they will not tolerate an incomes policy — agreed by all to be necessary — unless there is 'compensation' in the form of gradual transfer of control of industry and capital into the hands of the LO.

There is, then, a notable radicalization of the trade union movement which is parallel to that of the intelligentsia, but whereas the intelligentsia largely move outside the Social Democratic party as such, LO is inextricably tied to it. However, it is not the case that LO has a direct, formal influence on the government as it does in Sweden, where the leader of the LO is a Member of Parliament. This would seem inappropriate in Denmark, although it cannot be said whether it will always seem so.

The present government contains a far larger proportion of 'ideological' Social Democrats of the new, academic type than any hitherto. The effect of this will depend on many conditions, most of which are outside the government's control. There is at least a fair chance that a sensible and necessary incomes policy will be instituted without too much danger to the (inherently highly efficient) Danish industry. In my last section on general issues, below, I shall discuss the current and future effects of the 'ideological' Left in education, social policy and defence issues.

Sweden

The Swedish Social Democratic party is still formally called the 'Social Democratic Workers' Party', and it operates on a system of block memberships rather as does the British Labour party. Compared to the Danish party, it is certainly both much more highly centralized (and less democratic in its internal structure) and also much more closely tied to organized labour. In Denmark the Social Democratic party is not the only possible party of the working class; in Sweden, it still is. This is why the Social Democratic party there can still reasonably hope to obtain absolute majorities in Parliament, something which would be unthinkable in Denmark.

Another reason why in Sweden the Social Democratic party has obtained absolute majorities and still hopes to do so is the near-impossibility of forming new parties, which has prevented the outbreak of a Glistrup-type movement on the right and the proliferation of 'loose left' parties on the opposite flank. Sweden has had the same five parties for over sixty years, and there is no sign that this will change. They are the Communists, formerly pro-Moscow, but now Eurocommunist, opposed to nuclear power, and generally hospitable to the 'loose left' intellectuals who in Denmark have joined the newer parties; the Social Democrats; the liberal People's party, the Centre party and the conservative Moderate party. The much-discussed 'swing to the right' which has not really broken through in Denmark (unless you count Glistrup, which I would not, for reasons I cannot go into here) has in fact appeared in

Sweden, where the Moderates were the undoubted winners of this year's election, albeit at the expense of the other two non-socialist parties. Of course, the freedom of movement of any Swedish government is very limited by the absolutely untouchable public sector and, less tangibly, by the intense conformism and belief in established forms of the Swedish political culture.

This conformism and quite pronounced anti-individualism expresses itself in various ways. It has been brilliantly described by Roland Huntford in his book *The New Totalitarians*, which was published in Sweden also, but immediately denounced as misinformed and anti-Swedish. The reproach of being anti-Swedish is regularly levelled at anyone who dares to question the dominant ideology of the welfare state, the superiority of collective rights and ideals over individual wishes and rights, or in general any policy of the government. It is an efficient way to undercut serious political debate on ends and means, a phenomenon which is largely unknown in Sweden (unless you count marginal liberals like Lars Gustafsson). The result in terms of policy is that the paternal and interventionist state with its ethos of treatment and care of all citizens survives and grows, whether the government should happen to be Social Democratic or not.

Another concrete expression of conformism and the strong resentment of the new or the spontaneous is the fact that the established parties receive large subsidies from the state at election time with which to print ballot papers (in Sweden, each party prints its own ballot paper; the voter takes one from each party and fills in the one of his choice, discarding the rest; and it is not possible to give votes to individuals). However, any new party must pay for its own ballot papers and other campaign expenses. Clearly this is an extremely effective disincentive to new parties, and in fact no new party has appeared in parliamentary elections for a long time (although they proliferate at local elections, where the hindrances are less severe).

We have, then, a situation of great stability in the party-political spectrum, matched by equal or greater stability in the society itself. The power struggles and changes within the Social Democratic party are therefore of less importance, in that the particular personality of the leader and the colouring of the ideology of the dominant groups will be much less important than they are, say, in Great Britain. Nevertheless, the position and attitudes of the current leader, Olof Palme, are rather interesting. He has symbolized Scandinavian left-radical trendiness and intellectual anti-Americanism to the world at large, as for instance when he condemned Nixon's bombing of Hanoi in 1972 or, later, denounced CIA intervention in Chile. It is true that there is a strong trend of what would in Britain be considered extremely facile and modish leftism in Scandinavia, sanctioned in Sweden by the authority of Gunnar Myrdal, the economist who has for decades propounded an economic doctrine and a world-view hostile to liberalism and its claims. In many ways, Myrdal is the typical ancestor of the present wave of academic socialists, and there are many students of his in the current Social Democratic party. But what one must not forget is that all this posturing and seeming hypocrisy in foreign policy declarations (partly because Sweden plays a very minor role anyway and partly because Palme's denunciations never in fact affected e.g. the Swedish armaments industry and its trade with countries such as Chile or South Africa) was largely for use in domestic politics. Palme is probably committed in his way to his beliefs, but what is much more important for him is the prestige they give him or can give him at home. In this he is typical of Scandinavian politics: global issues play a very minor role, and the role they play is almost exclusively an instrumental one: 'See, I am maintaining the world's humanitarian and moral conscience; this proves the nobility and soundness of social democracy; vote for me.'

At the moment, having lost two elections in a row, Palme's position is less secure than it was. His academic intellectualism and flashy, overbearing manner with opponents he despises are beginning to cost him grassroots support. When this happens in a country as organized and placid as Sweden, things are seriously wrong. Contenders for the Social Democratic leadership include the current Chief Mayor of Stockholm, Jan-Ole Persson, a trade union man, and Lars Enquist, former leader of the Young Socialists and also much more in tune with the actual working class than Palme.

Sweden is to all intents and purposes a corporate state in which its own citizens believe. The formal rights − of free expression, of organization and of movement − are *not* guaranteed by the constitution, as this has always been regarded as 'unnecessary' (it would be 'anti-Swedish' to insinuate that a constitution which lacks the guarantees of formal freedom is not good enough for a country as civilized as Sweden). Furthermore, the top five thousand civil servants cannot be brought to court for abuse of power or office by any citizen, but only by the government; this is typical of the fundamentally authoritarian and bureaucratic structure of Swedish society.

Norway

I shall not say much about Norway, except that the Labour party has there been rather more radical for longer than either of the two major parties, because the Labour leader Einar Gerhardsen in the sixties carried through a struggle with the Communists for the allegiance of the left-radical intelligentsia and regionalists. In Norway, left-wing politics are associated with regionalism and nationalism, including support of the difficult 'New Norwegian' language, which was created out of old dialects in the mid-nineteenth century as a counterweight to the dominant language, which was basically Danish with a few local elements mixed in. The Danish of the towns and commercial classes has gradually become Norwegian, but it is still associated by the Left with conservatism and privilege, and therefore 'New Norwegian', which might otherwise be seen as a typical product of nineteenth-century romanticism and populism, has become a hallmark of Norwegian socialism. It is, to say the least, curious that an internationalist movement of the working class should in Norway adopt such extremely parochial and provincial attitudes. Partly this is because Norway did not have, until quite recently, a sizeable working class. It is a very fragmented country, communications are difficult and regionalism – including a strong tradition of decentralization – has always been strong. This is in many respects a good thing and is certainly one of the strengths of Norwegian society and the economy.

The 'swing to the right' manifested itself strongly in Norway at the local elections in 1979, in which the Conservative party, still trenchantly calling itself the Right, scored sensational gains on the local councils. Norway has been just as affected as Denmark and Sweden by the wave of radical and ideological educational and social theory, but it also seems as though the reaction there has been both swifter and more thorough. It seems at least possible that the Right will ultimately emerge as the largest party, larger even than the Labour party, which would create a unique and very interesting situation in Scandinavia.

General Issues

Education and Educational Policy
I have already referred to the radicalization of the intelligentsia and the advance of fashionable educational

theories in Scandinavia in the sixties and seventies. This has affected the social democratic parties in various ways. In Sweden, the Social Democratic government instituted far-reaching changes in school curricula and requirements in higher education in the mid-sixties. The consequences are now apparent: a rising rate of functional illiteracy, decreasing originality or competence of work in research and teaching and widespread dissatisfaction *also* among pupils. It was symptomatic of extreme concern in many sectors of the population when, in 1978, an association for the preservation of teaching standards in schools was formed with members across the entire political spectrum, from Jan Myrdal on the far Left to Lars Gustafsson on the moderate Right. Given the nature of Swedish society, an initiative of this kind betokens a phenomenal degree of worry and concern in the population at large. It remains to be seen whether it will have any effect on Social Democratic educational policies, although it does seem that there is a realization that pupils and students cannot be allowed to do what they want and that schools are not institutions to teach communication and solidarity, but institutions of learning, where certain necessary facts and abilities are taught, which are just as necessary under socialism as under capitalism.

In Denmark, the ideology of progressive education culminated in the U-90 plan, presented under the auspices of the then Minister of Education, Ritt Bjerregaard (now Minister of Social Policy and Welfare). The details of the plan are irrelevant here; suffice it to say that it represented the corporate, collectivist and anti-individualist ideology at its considerable worst. For example, it was clearly stated on several occasions that equality of result is more important than equal chances (because it guarantees collective solidarity and group harmony) and that, therefore, particularly bright or motivated children should be discouraged from learning and taught that their interests were 'unfair' to the others and should be suppressed. The plan caused a tremendous debate, which was also fuelled by the revelations of disaster which were just then leaking out from Sweden, where a policy of this type had already been in operation for a while. It seems that despite the strong tendency toward 'comprehensive' schooling and the gradual abolition of streaming, a certain degree of realism and a strong foundation of extremely competent teaching practice are still effective. On average, Danish secondary and higher education is of a very high standard, and would be even higher if everyone was not encouraged to enter secondary school and university, and it seems at least possible that the worst of the fashionable educational ideology has done its work. This is partly because it is commonly realized, also in the Social Democratic party, that a country such as Denmark, devoid of natural resources, possesses only one truly reliable resource, namely the intelligence of its inhabitants and their motivation to produce sound and saleable goods.

Trade Unions and Social Solidarity
In the world of politics and economics, the most important factor at present is the attitude of the unions and their federations, the LOs of Denmark, Sweden and Norway, to incomes policies and necessary restraints in a time of recession and uncertainty. In Norway, the LO accepted an eighteen-month absolute wage and price freeze, which held increases in 1979 to less than five per cent and has enormously improved productivity, employment and competitiveness (and brought down the national debt). Similar measures are being considered in Denmark, although it is clear that the LO will demand more in return than the Norwegian workers did. In Sweden, the situation has been largely allowed to slide, with the result that a potentially very serious crisis (of excessive costs, declining competitiveness and rising unemployment) faces Swedish

industry, traditionally far more reliant on heavy elements
– ships, cars, guns, aircraft – than Norwegian or Danish
industry.

The fundamental attitude of Danish workers, even
today, when group rights and wage differentials play a
much more prominent part than before, is still that 'the
smoke of one factory is as good as another's', that,
basically, productivity increases and industrial peace bring
more jobs and prosperity to all, and conflicts therefore are
not in anyone's interest. The attitude in Norway and
Sweden is similar (although individual unions in Sweden
are far more quiet than in Norway or Denmark), and there
is not a great deal of influence on the trade union
movement by the academic socialist intelligentsia, for
whom this set of attitudes constitutes blatant surrender to
the 'capitalists'.

Defence and Security Issues

I mentioned earlier that global, even European, policy,
plays a minute part in domestic debate in Scandinavia.
There is a high degree of indifference and/or naïveté as
regards issues such as NATO, the Soviet arms build-up,
strategic issues, the UN, and the Third World (assumed to
be universally noble and selfless, and deserving of the
benefit of the doubt in all cases). This being said, I must
add that in reality the military security of the Scandinavian
sector has in fact been guaranteed not least by a consensus
between the social democratic parties of Denmark,
Sweden, Norway and Iceland, all of which agree that
NATO and Western stability must be preserved in the
interests of the Scandinavian countries themselves. Even
neutral Sweden is part of this 'guarantee' inasmuch as,
neutral or not, the Swedish government is perfectly
capable of seeing who the potential aggressors in the
Scandinavian zone are; and they do not include the United
States.

The Soviet arms build-up and the increasing military activity in the Arctic sea has not had a significant effect on public debate, but it has definitely had an effect on the Scandinavian governments. Norway now allows non-national troops to participate in exercises north of Narvik, and Sweden has surreptitiously begun to consult with NATO concerning the possible Soviet threat. For instance, West German planes are allowed to fly over Sweden (technically 'violating' neutral air space), and the Swedish army has gradually made its equipment interoperable – within thirty minutes – with that of most NATO armies. Also, Sweden operates something called 'economic defence', which means maintaining all essential industries regardless of what sound market principles might dictate. Recently Danish shoe manufacturers found themselves inexplicably barred from the Swedish market; the reason was simply that the government wished to preserve the Swedish shoe industry in the event of war. The soldiers must be shod!

The concept of economic defence is not discussed much in Sweden or in the rest of Scandinavia, but there is no doubt that it is quite strictly adhered to. Sweden, of course, is fortunate in possessing both considerable raw materials and a well-developed military industry (planes, tanks, guns). Whatever the ideological colouring of the government, and however 'trendy' and radicalized the Social Democrats are, they remain committed to maintaining Swedish independence by all available means, including a deterrent military force. It is true that it has been considerably reduced from the mid-sixties when the Swedish air force actually had more active planes than the RAF, but this trend has stopped. There is undoubtedly at least as much naïveté about détente in Sweden as elsewhere, and the media often given the impression that the main danger to world peace comes from the 'capitalist' nations and especially from the United States. But underlying this is a high degree of realism and, increasingly, a measure of collaboration and consultation with NATO, which must be regarded as a sensible step in the circumstances.

In Denmark, lack of realism and the belief that it doesn't make any difference anyway what Denmark does is probably more widespread. The government remains uncommitted to the annual increase of three per cent in military spending desired by NATO, and new severe cuts in the armed forces, already relatively among the smallest in the alliance, are being considered. This has meant that the issue of the permanent presence of foreign troops has been raised again (though the possibility was immediately denounced as unrealistic and unacceptable by the government). The philosophy of the 'free ride' survives, although the population and the government are no longer honest enough to accept that they are getting a free ride and instead repeat the need for caution in assessing the 'alleged' Soviet threat, etc. The reaction of Western warnings against taking Brezhnev's offer of withdrawal of 20,000 troops from East Germany and dismantling a proportion of the medium-range ballistic missiles at face value was negative and there was a pervasive sense that the US and British pronouncements were made in bad faith ('of course, they have to support their own armaments industries'). At the same time, the number of 'political' conscientious objectors has fallen quite sharply, although this may have more to do with the high rate of unemployment and the better employability of a man who has done military service than with any renewed wave of patriotism. Public acceptance of NATO remains fairly high, and there is certainly no danger at all that Denmark should want to neutralize itself. But there is certainly also a considerable lack of realism, not only on the Left, in regard to the current European military balance and its significance.

Summary and Conclusion

I began this paper by asking whether the 'political culture' of the dominant social democratic parties had become more like that of the other parties; whether the 'exceptionalism' and desire for ultimate transformation of the political and economic system characteristic of the Scandinavian working-class parties (and of the German SPD until the Bad Godesberg programme) had been modified or strengthened in recent years. I then examined some trends and developments in the social democratic parties and in Scandinavian society at large: the growth of academic socialism and the rise of the radical intelligentsia, generally firmly anchored in the media, in education, in government service (and social work); the varying effects of the much-discussed 'swing to the right'; various attitudes to educational policy, defence, incomes policy etc. What can be concluded from these observations and considerations?

To a considerable extent, the choice of political culture, of exceptionalism versus participation on a par with other parties, has still to be made by Scandinavian social democracy. In Sweden, the party remains strongly tied to the working class and to organized labour via the system of block memberships and the strong loyalty of workers to the party. In Denmark, the struggle – much more quiet and less virulent than, say, in the British Labour party – between collectivist ideologues and reformist social democrats of the old school goes on, with time, apparently, favouring the leftists. A period of uneasy distance to the LO has temporarily ended with the realignment of the party along the lines of LO policy and LO plans for social and economic development (profit-sharing, gradual worker control, increased redistribution of incomes, inviolability of organizations and groups). In Norway, the Labour party successfully undercut leftist criticism at the cost of radicalizing itself and losing a great deal of territory on the right flank. This penalization of the party by the voters has not, seemingly, taken place in Denmark or Sweden (yet). At the same time, high social solidarity in Norway and a good deal of sound realism helped the Labour government to carry through a total wage and price freeze with the consent and cooperation of the LO, to such an extent that Norwegian productivity and competitiveness are in better shape now than for several years (of course, the inevitable demands for profit-sharing and compensation are now being made; one must admit that they make a lot more sense in a situation where in fact companies are doing much better than they are in Denmark, where there has been no wage and price freeze). All in all, ideological radicalism and academic influence coexist uneasily in all three parties with working-class, traditional elements (which can be more or less, usually less, radical) on the one hand, and on the other the 'older' generation of social democratic intellectuals of the Willy Brandt type. The choice has yet to be made, but it must be made soon in some form or other if the parties are not to face serious internal crises, possibly splits and certainly long-term decline, if only because the traditional voter base, the industrial workers, is declining in numbers.

In Denmark, the rise of the academics to prominence in the Social Democratic party occurred in the fifties. It was a process not without its problems and resentments, but fundamentally it was both necessary and accepted, because the party as the ruling party and the guarantor of social stability needed qualified specialists to run the country. The first academic at the top was the late Viggo Kampmann, who was only Prime Minister for a short time (1960-62), but who played a very important role for a number of years. His extroverted, self-ironic and utterly unselfconscious personality created to a large extent the myth of the 'sensible', responsible, friendly and intelligent Social Democratic politician. He was succeeded as leader by J. O. Krag, also an academic but a much more narrow and power-seeking person, less imaginative and in many ways less free. He in turn was succeeded − in 1973 − by the current leader and Prime Minister, Anker Jørgensen, who represents a break, in that he is not academic but a trade union man. However, his career has been in politics and Parliament, not in the LO. Thus he is a useful and convenient person, who has come to symbolize political experience as well as the necessary union ties. Unfortunately for the Danish economy, though, Mr Jørgensen, who enjoys great personal popularity and is undoubtedly a sincere and well-meaning man, does not seem able to conduct a consistent policy; after a half-hearted attempt to cooperate across the middle and separately from the LO, he has now forsworn collaboration with the 'bourgeois' parties and has once again aligned himself with organized labour.

In Sweden the party is still led by Palme, who is similar to Krag in his academic background, but different in his acceptance of the radical stance and fashionable views of the 'younger' intelligentsia. However, it seems that a challenge is building from the trade union movement, and it is far from unlikely that the Swedish party will also soon return to control by a representative of the organizations.

In Norway, the split between academics and old-timers has never been as pronounced as in Sweden or Denmark. Whereas the fact of a university degree was a cause for some suspicion in the old Danish party of the forties and fifties, such a fact in Norway is seen more in terms of the way in which it can serve the party (this was also how the Danish party gradually came to view the issue). The current Prime Minister and Labour leader, Oddvar Nordli, has a degree, but it does not mark him off from his trade union colleagues the way it would in the other countries.

In general, one can say that this split is now being surpassed in significance by another, which I have already referred to, namely that between reformists and ideologues. This is where the real confrontation will occur, if it does occur, and that is where the key to the future development of Scandinavia's three largest parties will lie.

In terms of political culture, it would also be fair to say that the place of the social democratic parties in the party system is less important now than the fact that the political culture of the societies as a whole has shifted since the early sixties and even since the early seventies. In the 1960 elections in Denmark the Social Democratic party explicitly campaigned on a theme of security and prosperity: social democracy as a guarantee of stability and increased prosperity. This theme could have been that of the Conservative party. Today, the Social Democratic parties in Sweden and Denmark no longer have 'liberty' as one of their programmatic aims: the manifesto of the Danish party was formerly entitled 'liberty, equality, fraternity'; it is now 'solidarity, equality and well-being' (the latter word is *trivsel*, an untranslatable Scandinavian term very popular in both Sweden and Denmark and referring to personality development and security, certainly, but also to a large extent to the 'correct' adaptation of the individual to the collective: no harmonious personality without alignment and acceptance of majority norms). This shift within social democracy is matched by a general shift in the society at large. Even the Moderates (conservatives) in Sweden cannot and will not undo the apparatus of the corporate welfare state built up under Social Democratic rule. The trends and debates within the major and minor parties on the Scandinavian Left must be seen against this background, which is familiar throughout Western Europe: a shift away from concern with real differences in ideas – liberalism versus socialism; state intervention versus free market economics etc. – to concern for the proper management of the extensive state as it is already installed. Hence also the almost total dominance of economic policy issues to the exclusion of what would, in earlier times, have been considered far more important, e.g. issues of foreign policy, defence and security and the 'final goals' of society. The final goals are no longer discussed, they – or the social democratic version of them – have been tacitly accepted. There are signs of a certain revival of interest here, but it should not be exaggerated. There is so little that (seemingly) can be done to stem the tide of organizational power (expressed, for instance, in immediate illegal strikes if employers change wage differentials) or reduce the massed weight of the state with its innumerable agencies and institutions, staffed by increasingly self-righteous and radicalized bureaucrats – the new social democratic voters. At the same time, it would be wrong to exaggerate these problems (for they are problems). The Scandinavian countries remain open societies; that is not the issue. The issue is rather whether anybody is still bothered to make use of that fact.

CHAPTER NINE

Europe and America

LUIGI BARZINI

Behind the movement towards European union lie fears of the growing strength of the Soviet Union. A further impetus comes from the fear that Europeans have of themselves. We Europeans have made so many mistakes, have gone through so many catastrophes, have believed so many spuriously charismatic leaders, have gone into such demented wars over so many centuries that, although you won't read it or find it in magazines and books, it is there all the same – you must not underestimate the Europeans' fear of Europeans. A further factor is fear of the United States. Though perhaps fear isn't quite the right word – anxiety, apprehension, doubt may be more accurate terms. One day General De Gaulle remarked bluntly to the Italian President Saragat: 'You can't trust the Americans!' The President, taken aback at these words, defended the Americans. A few weeks later something happened and the President commented to me, with a shrug: 'The General was right after all.'

However, in my experience, what causes problems between the United States and Europe is not that Americans cannot be trusted, but rather that Europeans do not understand Americans or America. Perhaps that is not so surprising, as Americans have rarely understood themselves!

In a chapter of necessarily restricted length it is difficult

to eviscerate one of the deepest enigmas of the present time
– what is the United States? Those who have little real
knowledge of America will automatically say it is a great
nation, the greatest nation of all time, and now a reluctant
empire. Can it be denied that America is a great nation? It
behaves like one in emergencies (who can forget the
reaction to Pearl Harbor?), and at dramatic moments in
history Americans act with a unity associated with the
ancient nations of Western Europe. Yet the doubts remain.
Can it truthfully be said that the inhabitants of that vast
area of land (a country the size of Europe) form a nation?

I remember the day I called on the Italian foreign
minister during a period when he was involved in difficult
negotiations with America. He explained that, from
various sources, he had been able to deduce what the
Americans were planning to do. 'What are these sources?'
I asked. It transpired that the President of the United
States had said one thing, a prominent general another and
the influential *New York Times* something else. 'From this
our ambassador has deduced an overall, coherent, logical
design,' the minister informed me. I listened sceptically.
'Maybe you're right,' I said, 'perhaps such a design does
exist, but then again, perhaps it doesn't. It doesn't
automatically follow that, because the President said one
thing, the *New York Times* another and the general yet
another, there exists an agreement, a plan or a vast design.
That is not the way Americans work.' The minister was
rather perplexed by this. He said: 'Isn't there a centre
where everything is planned?' 'There's the White House,' I
replied, 'but it is a rather strange place. The day before the
new President is due to take over, the retiring President
takes away every piece of paper in the building. There are
no files, no permanent officials – except one. When the
newly sworn-in President reaches the Oval Office he rings
a bell and the butler appears. In this famous building,
housing the most powerful elected official in the world,

only the butler can proudly claim to be a permanent official!'

The poor President! He has worked so hard and for so long to become President that he knows little more about the subject of foreign affairs than what he has been able to gather from the newspapers. He has to spend long hours being briefed by experts on what has gone before and what must be done in the future. Such a way of ordering things seems odd to the European mind. When a government changes in Britain, France or Italy, life goes on much as before because the papers are there, the officials are there, continuity is guaranteed. But a new President of the United States takes months to realize how to get things done.

As I explained this to the minister his face turned pale with fright! 'How can we negotiate if we do not know what they are up to?' he asked nervously. 'How can they possibly get anything done?'

Once again we return to the core of the problem, the enigma of American nationhood. Those who have a deep knowledge of America are aware that it is a conglomeration of people of diverse origin, different races, different cultures and different beliefs, even more diversified because they live in such a vast country, that climatically goes from the cold of Scandinavia to the heat of North Africa. So what is it that keeps Americans together? If one studies American history and talks to Americans, one eventually realizes that there are few bonds of unity. In fact, Americans can be likened to iron filings held together by magnetic waves and given a shape, rather than held tightly in place. The main characteristic which provides Americans with such shape is American ideology and philosophy. Americans know they have a mission in history, which is that of being the model of the new world and society to come. They must build a more perfect society, they must improve everything in sight (including pasta!). They believe in the perfectibility of man, in continual progress; they are building (so they believe) the new Jerusalem.

The idea of the new Jerusalem is very old in the United States. It goes back centuries, surely to the founding of the country itself, to the establishment of the independent Republic. The 'Founding Fathers' were obsessed with the idea. Why? I have discussed this with numerous American historians. They say that this feeling of mission to create a better society has been with their ancestors since the seventeenth century; and one suggested that perhaps it was a method by which Protestants who had found shelter in the United States excused themselves for not being present at the religious wars taking place in Europe during the period of early settlement. There may well be some truth in this. Yet whatever its origins, this belief that everything can be improved, that life will get better, that tomorrow will dawn a better day, remains a truly American obsession. It is often called the American civic religion – it can become the American dream. This forms the dynamic force which holds Americans together and makes the Republic march with confidence towards a better future – not only for themselves, but for the whole world. Thomas Jefferson said: 'America is the world's best hope,' and so it is, because these hopes are not just the hopes by Americans for America. As a matter of fact, the American experiment developed from eighteenth-century European (French and English) philosophies, and the hopes generated at that time are not only America's, not only Europe's, but the hopes of all men all over the world.

So perhaps we can conclude that America is not a nation as we conceive nations in Europe but an experiment in the creation of a better society. Yet such a final answer would be mistaken, for sometimes America is not even wholly that; sometimes it is something quite different. There is one quality of the American character which fights against idealism. It is pragmatism. The job has to be done, has to be done well and quickly, whatever its nature. Sometimes, as a result, Americans find themselves supporting dubious dictators supplying them with weapons and advisers, and these dictators and regimes do not meld with the American dream, the idealism, with the noble sentiments that inspired America for many decades. But the job has to be done and so Americans are forced to put up with reality. In short, America is a crusading country, animated by idealism, mitigated by pragmatism.

America is a complicated puzzle. I would say that the pragmatic urge makes the very existence of problems insufferable for Americans. Americans cannot live with the idea that there are problems waiting to be solved. Recently an eminent American journalist came to see me in Rome and I explained to him all the problems of the contemporary Italian political situation. He looked at me with consternation and said: 'What is the solution, Luigi?' I said: 'Dear fellow, let us think. Suppose we are in Constantinople, the Turks are attacking, almost climbing over the walls and you turn to the Emperor and say: "Emperor, what is the solution?" The answer may be that there is no solution.'

I wrote earlier that the American dream is *our* dream and that is why we Europeans often feel a special affinity for the United States. We are on the same wavelength, we hope for the same things, which can be summed up in the one word 'liberty'. Not, however, the liberty which says that a man should be free to do anything that pleases him, but liberty in the sense of the responsibility of the autonomous man who is aware of belonging to a society. This is real liberty, the liberty of Europeans, the liberty of Americans, the idea for which so many Europeans and Americans died in wars in the last two centuries. So the dream is shared; it is also ours.

But there is one American quality which can sometimes

make collaboration with them a source of anxiety. It is a curious aspect of the American character, one which I have explored without coming up with an answer. The quality is impatience. All travellers to the US since the eighteenth century have talked about Americans being in a hurry, rushing here and there. I don't know if, in reality, Americans are more in a hurry than others. Trains and waiters are very slow, drivers drive more slowly than Italians, but this idea that Americans are impatient, impetuous, has been preserved and passed on for two centuries, so there may be something in it. Why are Americans in a hurry? I discussed this matter with Walter Lippmann once, and we tried various answers and could not come up with a definitive one. So I give you two hypotheses.

They are in a hurry because life with its problems is intolerable and they know each problem has an answer and if every problem has an answer, why not reach it today, tomorrow morning at the latest and, as one of the most famous American flour mills has as its own motto: Eventually Why Not Now? So, 'Eventually why not now?' could be written on the coat of arms of the United States. Very often Americans do, in fact, get results very quickly; but sometimes they rush into complicated, seemingly intractable, situations, when it would be wiser to wait a while and study. I have witnessed this impatience several times during my lifetime. Part of my youth was spent in the United States and, during this time, a constitutional amendment and law had forbidden the production, transportation and consumption of alcoholic beverages. Result: there was an enormous increase in drunkenness and lawlessness. The changes in the law had not been properly thought out or the possible effects sensibly examined. They rushed into the future, towards the better world of tomorrow, much too soon. More recently, in Italy, just a few years ago, I saw the Americans give all the help they could to the creation of the Centre-Left administration, which would solve all Italy's problems by isolating the Communists. Events did not turn out as planned. Within a few years Italy was on the verge of bankruptcy, the Communists were more powerful than ever before, and the state decayed to such an extent that it will take a generation to reconstruct, if ever. I could give other examples. But the aims of Americans are always noble and generous, forms of ambition for a better world, towards the solution of problems.

The other hypothesis is a rather different one. We in Europe tend to think in terms of families and generations – if I don't get rich I hope my son will, or even my grandson. Somehow Americans think in terms of individuals. Life is a short trip in the light between two infinite darknesses and everything has to be accomplished before sunset, within one lifetime, before a man dies – the political reform, the family fortune, the achievement of great missions. Perhaps this is why Americans are always in such a hurry. Yet, whatever the cause, it is this impatience which so often makes dealing with the Americans so difficult.

What does all this mean for America's position in the world? Are the Americans isolationists or interventionists? American historians have pondered long and deep over this crucial question so that, for a time, the 'isolationist' school of thought appears to have convinced almost everybody, but then the 'interventionist' school hits back, then it is the turn of the 'isolationist' school again, and so the debate goes on. I would suggest that, far from being in conflict, for Americans isolationism and interventionism are two sides to the same coin. The Americans' sense of mission, their desire to improve man's lot on earth, makes them want to teach other people better ways of governing themselves, better ways of producing wealth, sharing wealth, distributing wealth, all with the aim of lessening the danger to the peace of the world. Sometimes Americans become impatient because people aren't prepared to listen to what appears to them as obvious good sense, so they take up arms. In the past, they did this more often. They landed marines in banana republics; one of the most idealistic of Americans, President Woodrow Wilson, ordered cavalry divisions to cross the Rio Grande. It is so obviously clear to Americans that their way is the best way for men to govern themselves and reach peaceful social conditions — so why won't others readily follow their example? It is almost as if other countries do not *want* to understand; so Americans think: 'We will send the arms and do it for them.' So I would suggest that the dichotomy is that they are fundamentally isolationists by preference; when they are interventionists they are impatient isolationists who want to get the involvement over as quickly as possible.

America has a tremendous capacity to influence men's minds and lives in all manner of ways. A couple of years ago Americans 'discovered' a new French kitchen utensil that did everything except sweep the floor. So many Americans bought this machine that the company in France that manufactured it became an immense industry and had competitors investing billions of francs and building enormous factories everywhere. Now, the day may arrive when Americans will say: 'To hell with this machine, let's try another one.' Entire provinces of France would be plunged in despair, demonstrations erupt, people weep in the streets. At the end of the sixties many students in Europe demonstrated against the Vietnam war, even though they were not directly involved. They filled the squares and the streets with their banners protesting against someone else's war; nowadays, Europeans are jogging like President Carter. America has this capacity to involve others in her way of life.

In conclusion, I will admit that no nation is coherent,

logical, predictable − not even a totalitarian one. I have lived in a totalitarian country and, when you have an opportunity to observe it closely, everything appears inchoate, disorderly and contradictory. When seen from the outside it may seem a solid, monolithic society, but in reality no nation possesses such a coherence. But to Europeans the United States is a problem because of the realization that the future depends upon knowing what the Americans will be doing tomorrow. Think of Kaiser Wilhelm of Germany and of Hitler. They both believed what they were told, that the Americans were isolationist and not interested in Europe's wars. They both lost in the end because they were so ill-informed. Or take the North Koreans. They read in an American newspaper that, in the case of an attack, the United States would not defend South Korea. Well, some of the longest and bloodiest wars in the world came about through misjudging the American character.

In the decade of the 1980s, the United States, historically, geographically, militarily and politically, holds such an important position that we should know which tack it is going to take next, what it will decide next, how it sees the world and its role in it, and how these perceptions are both arrived at and are likely to change.

Never in the history of the world has the future of so many people depended on the behaviour of one nation or, shall we say, on the clear knowledge by foreigners of that nation's mood and decisions.

CHAPTER TEN

America and Europe

DAVID BOWEN

The founding of NATO in 1949 constituted a recognition that the political and military alliance which had defeated Hitler was not sufficient to address the problems of post-war Europe. After years of destruction and death a battered Europe was apparently not to receive the era of peace which it needed for recovery and growth but instead the threat of another war. Thirty years later that danger still remains, but those thirty years of peace have been underwritten by NATO. The Atlantic alliance continues to remain the bedrock upon which the peace and stability of Europe are built.

From my own perspective as a Member of the US Congress and particularly of the House Foreign Affairs Committee, I would like to give you an observation or two about how Congress, and particularly the House of Representatives, which is certainly the more sensitive of the two chambers to changing public moods, views the Atlantic partnership. For most Americans Europe is still viewed as the most important part of the globe — economically, politically, and militarily. We retain a deep cultural affinity for Europe. How else could it be? Our nation grew from the perilous explorations of Europeans and the social, political and economic thought and action of Europeans who came here in search of a better life, to create a more perfect society, or to escape persecution.

The European connection continually reasserts itself, not only in our involvement in two great European wars, but also in the post-Second World War experience which led to the founding of NATO. Those immediate post-war years left an indelible mark on the mind of the American people. To Americans it was an era when a crisis almost equal to that of the Second World War, but which did not break out into war, was taking place in Europe, when Europe faced a challenge to its economic and political survival, when its existence and its established democracies were threatened by outside military might, when Europe was perceived even more than in the Second World War as being the first line of defence for the United States, since communism seemed even more aggressively determined to conquer the entire globe than did Nazism and Fascism.

Those traumatic years have coloured our vision of the world ever since, but as we now move into the fourth decade of NATO we have experienced a series of crises at other points around the globe, and we have seen Europe become stronger and more stable as other areas became more unstable. We have seen our fears realized that Soviet communism would attempt to do just what it had always proclaimed it intended to do, as it expanded politically, economically and militarily into every region and continent.

We have fought two wars in Asia and have coped with the problem of communist domination in China and for the time being turned it to our own purposes. We have faced continuing strife in the Middle East and the problems − along with Europe − of decolonization in Africa and Asia. In addition, we have seen the development of Japan into the third economic power of the world and our number two trading partner, behind Canada.

Despite all of these events, along with the Soviet

invasion of Afghanistan and American hostages in Tehran, I cannot really say that non-European or North-South problems have replaced Europe in American thinking. It is simply that we have a new dimension in our international thinking, a more global perspective. It is not that the problems of other regions are of greater concern than those of Europe, but it is a matter of perceiving that there are other problems and there are other regions. Whereas in the immediate post-war years Europe was for most Americans — though certainly not all — the only important region of foreign policy concern, it is now the first in a long list of foreign policy concerns.

A quarter of a century ago when I graduated from Harvard and came to Europe to study, it seemed the natural thing to do. I suspect if I were to do the same today, I might consider going to Japan, though I would probably still come here to England. The American attitude today is, I feel, more a matter of broader horizons than greater distance from Europe.

I believe that most Members of Congress, reflecting as we do the communications and pressures of our constituents, feel that the post-war concern for Europe, our 'Eurocentrism', is no longer as acute or as immediate as it was in the days of the Berlin airlift. Afghanistan is today's Berlin airlift. In fact, ironically, there is a great similarity between the Berlin airlift and some of the crises of East-West relations in recent years, in which we were able to provide moral and perhaps economic support to a people but were unable or unwilling to take military action.

Unquestionably, America retains a deep commitment to Europe and to the Atlantic alliance, and that commitment I do not expect to see diminished. Understandably, at the same time, there is apprehension about the possibility of a Western European government with representation in it which could create security problems for the Atlantic alliance. Americans continue to be concerned about activities of the extreme Left in Europe, their strength in trade unions and political parties, and the subject of Eurocommunism continues to be a lively one in our country.

Perhaps we do, as many suggest, overreact to the phenomenon of European communist political strength. We are, in fact, impressed with the ability of Western European political leaders to restrict the political advances of Marxism and to maintain good relations between the United States and Europe. And, in any event, the radicalization of some left-of-centre parties in Europe is not a phenomenon which has as yet stricken apprehension into the hearts of Americans, either because of ignorance of this development on our part or the fact that many of these developments have taken place outside of government majorities. I feel confident the American-European relationship will endure no matter what particular stresses are placed on it from time to time.

One of the fundamental developments which I have seen in my own constituency and which I believe characterizes American thinking during the last thirty years has been the development of a sustained interest in foreign policy matters. The worldwide trade involvement of our nation and our global political and military commitments have penetrated to every walk of life in the United States. The process of education and, in fact, the realization of our global responsibilities has been largely successful, and a normal post-war shift to isolationism has been halted. This is, in my opinion, a process that will not be reversed. An era of détente and accommodationism did not change this, and it is not likely to change as we move into what appears to be a new period of confrontationism.

It is important, however, for our allies to realize that we in the United States have discovered in recent years that we are mortal economically. We have energy problems, balance of payment problems, inflation and unemployment problems that we have been unable to solve. I know that Europe has these problems as well, but the gap has been closed strikingly between American and European economic strength during the last thirty years, and Americans consequently expect our Atlantic allies to support a larger proportion of the burden of defence and assistance to less-developed nations. I feel that many of us concerned about maintaining strong Atlantic ties hope that our European friends can move in this direction, especially in light of the post-Vietnam trauma which has made it so difficult for us to come to grips with Soviet expansionism and adventurism in recent years.

In this respect, let me say that I believe that President Carter has begun to turn the corner in the development of a more realistic foreign policy, one that appreciates Soviet policy for what it is, and that he will construct American foreign policy accordingly. At least the words sound good so far, and we will await the development of clear and consistent actions to fit the words.

As to the perception of many Americans that we are trying to shoulder the burdens of defence and development alone, I know that Europeans who are carrying a substantial tax burden for defence and foreign assistance may feel a bit put out at this view, but until that burden is comparable to the one imposed upon American taxpayers and American industrial competitiveness, it will continue to be an issue.

The concern of the American people is not so much one of precisely measuring the amount of such contributions as it is to sense that the support and cooperation which we receive from our Atlantic allies for mutually beneficial policies is sufficient so that the American people do not feel − correctly or incorrectly − that the Europeans are perfectly willing to let us fight the Cold War against the Soviets and defend the values and interests which we hold in common while they enjoy the economic and fiscal benefits of détente.

In terms of this kind of cooperation, I would like to make a point or two about NATO and the weapons systems which concern us all. The fact that the SALT II treaty has been signed – even though in my opinion the United States Senate is unlikely to ratify it – indicates considerable awareness in the US that some kind of parity has been attained in terms of strategic weaponry, whether or not the treaty is sound and would do as much for a strategic balance as does the present state of affairs. This event requires of necessity greater attention to be focused upon intermediate weaponry and the question of how the European NATO nations will respond to this Soviet weapons challenge. So far, there have been welcome signs of what appears to us a reasonable and responsible European response to the Soviet build-up of SS-20 missiles. West Germany has indicated a willingness to accept land-based Cruise and Pershing II missiles on its territory as a part of a coordinated response to this Soviet build-up, and Britain and Italy have also acted affirmatively. Others hopefully will as well, and it is this kind of response by our European allies that is so badly needed to help cement our continuing commitment to the alliance.

There is ongoing argument as to whether the dual approach is still the right one, that is, whether we need to persevere with world arms control systems such as SALT II while at the same time we develop more defence and strike capability in other weapons systems. We know that some on the Left in Western Europe are opposed to this two-track approach, pinning their faith instead solely upon arms control as a means of preserving cordial East-West relations. But we take heart that the majority of Western European opinion, including the major governments of Western Europe, seems to realize the importance of NATO possessing the necessary arms to deter a direct threat of

Soviet forces moving into Western Europe.

I believe that most of my colleagues in the Congress hold a strong opinion that while American nuclear capability may be the ultimate deterrent against Soviet aggression, no one can be certain about the response of a given administration in Washington under every conceivable circumstance to a Soviet attack on Europe and that therefore our European allies would be well advised to integrate these new intermediate range weapons into Western Europe's defence system. As we all know, the more precise weapons which the Soviets have now developed, particularly the SS-20 missiles, enable them to focus more accurately upon specific military targets without jeopardizing major population centres, and this calls for a response in kind from Western Europe. In short, intermediate weaponry is absolutely essential for Europe's own protection, and the case for it needs to be established here in Europe even more certainly than in the United States.

Looking beyond weapons systems, there is a growing body of thought in the US which argues that NATO needs to be restructured or reoriented so that it can concern itself with problems on a broader range of areas than simply that of Europe. I feel that in light of the growing global perspective which I have already described to you on the part of the Congress and the American public, such a development could make NATO into a more effective organization and bring it more into line with the realities of current geopolitics. I am well aware that European nations have their own commitments in other parts of the world and in many instances are performing very effectively in pursuit of their own and Western interests. Even so, I feel that North Atlantic strength could be much greater if the allies could develop a joint approach which might emanate from NATO in addressing problems in other parts of the world. With the departure of SEATO and CENTO there appears to be an organization gap or an alliance gap which needs to be filled, whether by expanding the responsibilities within the current structure of NATO or by expanding NATO into a global alliance which could serve as a more comprehensive and more effective coordinating body for military and economic defence against Soviet expansion.

The events in Afghanistan and Iran point up the importance of some coordinated approach on the part of NATO nations in dealing with events outside of Europe, events which have been profoundly disturbing in the United States and which have left us with a feeling of deep apprehension about the possibility of having to face such crises alone.

Economically, I feel very optimistic about the attitude of the American people toward Europe. The Common Market is viewed as a worthy competitor as well as one with whom we will continue to do extremely good business. We are quite pleased with the recent conclusion of the Tokyo Round of the Multilateral Trade Negotiations and feel that it should help substantially in the expansion of trade with Europe. Such trade ties should help develop, expand and perfect the concept of mutual security which has been established in NATO.

Finally, I would like to address the importance of maintaining increasing contacts between America and Europe. It is imperative that we understand each other in the face of potentially dangerous Soviet-Western confrontations which we have seen recently. Hopefully, the new economic strength of Europe and the now comparatively reasonable cost of travel in the United States will stimulate a great many more Europeans to visit us and counterbalance the heavy flow of Americans who have for so many years streamed into Europe.

With such contacts we may be less likely to arrive at a 'European view of the world' or an 'American view of the world' and, short of the millennium at least, arrive at a Western, a democratic, or a non-communist view of the world. Certainly, we can on both sides of the Atlantic perceive that mutual cooperation and defence are essential to our mutual prosperity and survival.

CHAPTER ELEVEN

American Opinion and Perceptions of Political Change in Europe

ROY GODSON

This paper briefly describes American perceptions of political change in Europe. It also will describe briefly what the United States is and is not doing – and what might be done. The focus will be on the present administration rather than the Congress, and also on several important non-governmental sectors, particularly organized labour and the attentive academic community.

United States Government

The basic commitment of the United States toward Western Europe remains unchanged. For the US government – and, indeed, for US public opinion – Europe is still the most important area of the world. But the US government and the American people overall are crisis-oriented. Two or three years ago, in the mid-seventies, American attention was riveted on Europe, particularly on internal changes in the European Left which many believed would bring communists and socialists into much more powerful positions. There was also considerable focus on the modernization of NATO forces in view of the Soviet build-up.

Today, Americans are preoccupied with other problems

and regions of the world. Growing Soviet strategic power and the Soviet ability to project its forces into the Middle East, Asia and even Africa has become the dominant concern in the US national security establishment.

United States officials no longer view Europe as a crisis area. The threat of 'Eurocommunism' is perceived to have receded. With the election of Margaret Thatcher and the increased strength of conservatives on both the national and European levels, many now perceive that Europe is being swept by 'Euro-Conservatism'. Relatively few people are worried now about communists coming into government in any southern European state or are alarmed, if aware, of the leftward currents within the social democratic parties of northern Europe.

Hence, American officials, who were scrambling to try to prevent communists from entering governments in the mid-seventies, are no longer occupying themselves with the evolution of European change. Conversations with senior US officials in Washington and American embassies throughout Europe tend to confirm this conclusion. In addition, the US is not mobilizing resources or instruments to significantly effect European developments. After some effort to galvanize and coordinate Euro-American policy towards OPEC and energy, US interest has fallen off. The US government also has placed some additional funds at the disposal of officials who want to promote greater Euro-American cooperation on the political/cultural level, but relatively little political planning and effort have gone into this endeavour.

There is nothing in the US like the German political foundations to promote long-term political objectives on a non-governmental level which, in turn, would influence intergovernmental policy. This country does not have foundations like the Friedrich Ebert or the Konrad Adenauer to promote political/cultural change in other countries, and the US has given up attempts to influence political change covertly in other countries. The demise of the CIA's covert action sections in the early seventies, which has now been well documented in the US, also means we are engaging in hardly any open or covert effort to effect political change in Europe.

The Non-governmental Sector

The academic elite, or 'the brightest and the best', long ago downgraded the threat to democracy in Western Europe from either the Soviet Union or the anti-democratic Left on the Continent. Nevertheless, many American academics are interested in the evolution of the European Left. A few years ago they were delighted with the rise of Eurocommunism and the likelihood that communist parties would enter government. Indeed, many insisted that Southern Europe was ungovernable without communists in government.

Recently, these 'specialists' in European affairs have begun to shift their attention to European socialists, or what some of them conceive to be 'Eurosocialism', and to socialist and communist trade union organizations. They still hope that somehow the Left, whether the socialists or the communists, will emerge as the dominant force in the future and they try to maintain personal contact with them.

American trade union leaders continue to believe that the Soviet Union and the communist Left in Europe present both short-term and long-term dangers to democracy and free trade unions in both Europe and the US. For over forty years American labour has worked to prevent anti-democratic elements both on the right and on the left from acquiring control of the Continent. The AFL-CIO, the main body of American trade unions, continues to press the United States Government to modernize US forces, as well as the forces in Europe. It also urges the

Western governments to cooperate more closely in developing policies to deal with the economic/political threat and problems posed by OPEC and other forces that would deprive the West of raw materials at reasonable prices.

American labour also has urged the US government to assist democratic forces in Southern Europe in withstanding the efforts of Soviet-backed communist parties to take over the trade union movement and other organizations they believe vital for the success of democracy.

In recent years, as George Meany became increasingly old and ill, the Federation did not do as much as it had in the past to implement its own policy. With the advent of a new leadership and changes in the organization of the AFL-CIO's international affairs staff, it can be expected that American labour once again will become a significant player in cooperation with counterpart unions in Western Europe. The US government and the AFL-CIO will reenter the ILO – and it seems likely that the AFL-CIO will establish much closer ties, and may even rejoin, the International Confederation of Free Trade Unions.

The American business community has not developed coherent policies to deal with political change in other areas of the world. American business appears to be continuing on its merry way, on the assumption that somehow the US government will make the world safe for American capitalism.

What Ought to be Done

Unfortunately, the American government's vision of Europe is blurred and, like other aspects of American policy, somewhat chaotic. The US needs to analyse specific trends in Europe and decide on a long-term – or even a medium-term – strategy to support the evolution of democratic forces in Europe and other parts of the world. At the same time, it should be noted that the US government is open to being influenced. Because there is no coherent analysis and strategy, those with concrete programmes now have an opportunity to influence the policymakers.

Organized labour, in my view, should be doing much more to implement its own policy. American labour has provided some moral support to assist democratic forces in Southern Europe, but hopefully it can do more on the organizational and material levels, albeit in close cooperation with European organizations.

Those intellectuals who understand that European communists pose a long-term threat to democracy, especially in view of increasing Soviet power, must begin to work together on a transatlantic basis. It is not useful to decry the danger and then to do almost nothing except write articles and bemoan our fate. Intellectuals may not be the best organizers in the world, but they are not without organizational skills.

Finally, the Europeans themselves must demonstrate to Americans that they want the US to remain involved in Western Europe. The European governments must demonstrate that they are willing to undertake additional burdens either in Europe or in other parts of the world to maintain our common freedom. In addition, they also have to actively and persistently request American involvement in European affairs. Conservatives in Europe should press conservatives in the United States; centrists and social democrats in Europe should address their counterparts in the United States; European trade unionists, businessmen and intellectuals should actively search out their counterparts, determine areas of common interest and actively work together to promote values of common concern.

There is so much to do and so much that can be done.

CHAPTER TWELVE

The Alliance under Stress: National Interests and Political Change

DOUGLAS EDEN

Western Europe remains geographically, politically and ideologically weak, not yet recovered from two world wars. Its countries are concerned, in the foreign policy field, primarily with the division of their own continent and none are capable of intervening further afield than Africa or the Near East if at all.

The appeasement mentality originally derived from the traumas of the first war can still be identified among many West European supporters of détente today. Perhaps more important, however, is the damage done by the last war and its aftermath to the foundation of European organization and moral strength, the nation-state.

The values of Europeans have evolved through hundreds of years of national histories and are inseparable from the national experiences and sensibilities which produced them. They are not dependent on legal documents nor presented as principles of necessarily universal application. A European who denies his nationality effectively cuts himself off from the moral and ethical anchorages which are part of his personal identity.

The expression of pride in one's nation has been difficult

for most Europeans since 1945. The shades of Fascism and Nazism, the victory of Soviet communism and the consequent progress of international Marxism, the imperial decay of the post-war years, all have conspired to suppress the spiritual revival of the European nations in the West. This has increased their vulnerability to the ideology and power which suppresses Europe in the East and actively works to subvert their national institutions, their independence and their adherence to the Western alliance.

At the same time, the alliance of which they are members and the United States which leads it have had no forward policy since the admission in 1956 that the 'rollback' policy envisaging the eventual liberation of Eastern Europe was a fraud. The American withdrawal to a defensive posture in Europe and her consequent preoccupation elsewhere, encouraged and diverted by the Soviet Union, exacerbated the underlying weakness of West European morale.

Yet, at no time have German, French or Italian governments viewed themselves or their countries' interests in other than national terms. Aware that the United States and their neighbours regarded their nationalisms with suspicion and disfavour as the kindling for two world wars, they formed the European Economic Community ostensibly to submerge these nationalisms. In fact, the EEC provides an acceptable channel for the pursuit of national objectives. Americans who promoted the EEC as a putative United States of Europe operated under a massive misconception if they really believed their coordinate state system could be translated to Europe. Britain and France remain nations, Massachusetts and Louisiana merely states. The EEC has accordingly evolved into a useful and legitimate cover for the prosecution of national foreign policies by various member countries.

The net effect of the EEC on the Atlantic alliance has

been divisive. The Western liberal economic order, including its GATT/OECD trading system, is part of the foundation of Western security, and the trading system is subjected to disruption by the formation of internecine trading blocks. Against whom was it thought the EEC would raise tariffs and protect its members' trading positions – the Soviet Union?

Now the looming recession puts further stress on Western unity by increasing pressure in Europe for import controls. This is serious enough as contemplated by individual nations, but its potential for increasing protectionism on an EEC scale magnifies the threat to the liberal economic order and thus to the cohesion of the alliance. It must be said that the anti-American Left, which is the only European political element currently fully committed to such a policy, is still a long way from being the dominant voice in the EEC (although its prospects within some of the member nations are rather better). Nevertheless, increased economic tension contributes to the fundamental conflict between European-centred nationalism and American universalism which provides a lever for Soviet policymakers and the anti-NATO Left in Western Europe to manipulate and undermine the Atlantic system.

The country under greatest stress from this conflict is probably Germany, situated on the front line of the alliance. No country's sense of nationality has been under greater assault, yet none has as tangible a motivation to fight for survival. Her former chauvinism bears the indictment for two world wars and she could expect no sympathy for her post-war dismemberment. Even after 35 years, the successors to the Reich, no matter how self-effacing, pacific and respectable, still must contend with the physical consequences. The German people are already resigned to the permanent alienation of one third of their country (mainly in compensation to Poland for the half of that country the Soviets took). Another third is held hostage and the remaining third shelters the refugees evicted or escaped from the alienated or occupied territories. Having accepted the Oder-Neisse line, the German people would like at least to reunite what remains recognizably German.

Of all the Western nations, Germany is the only one with a territorial problem. Such problems form the clearest of national interests, most likely to motivate a calculated and coherent diplomatic strategy.

As long as the West appeared to have a forward policy and rollback was on the agenda, complete reliance on the alliance and uncompromising hostility to the East (e.g. the Hallstein Doctrine) were the order of the day for the free German state. The order began to change as it was gradually understood that the Austrian treaty of 1955 and allied inaction over Hungary in 1956 signified American and allied unwillingness to risk tension over the status quo in Eastern Europe, least of all for the sake of German reunification. As the American posture changed, increasing stress placed on the hostage position of West Berlin promoted the adjustment of German attitudes and perceptions to the new circumstances.

Thus, if the Soviet Union provided the seeds of détente and the United States, albeit unwittingly, sowed them, German soil nourished and brought forth the plant.

West Germany sees her objective now as distant, to be approached gradually with the aid of time; so, subtly and patiently, she operates both an Ostpolitik and a Westpolitik rather in the tradition of Bismarck. The American alliance has priority, for the security of the third of Germany which remains free must be uppermost. However, as opinion polls ceaselessly show, Germans overwhelmingly believe that reunification can only be achieved by promoting an opening to the East. No one in Bonn appears to know precisely how the Ostpolitik will reunite the nation, but the long-term Bismarckian view is that anything which could set back reduction in tension, gradual increase in contact and concert with the East and steady movement toward a possible agreement by the Soviets to reunification (even in thirty or forty years' time) should be avoided.

German public opinion is so strong on this question – and reinforced by the benefits achieved by Ostpolitik thus far – that any strategic difference between the political parties is limited by electoral considerations. The 1980 federal elections will not change the basic thrust of German foreign policy. Only external influences, such as a hardening and clarity in American foreign policy, can do that.

A CDU/CSU government under Herr Franz Josef Strauss might attempt to reduce Ostpolitik to mere insistence on observance of the existing treaties, but it is questionable whether it could resist pressure to continue the process of accommodation with the East, particularly if the American commitment carries less and less conviction. At the same time, the Social Democratic Chancellor, Herr Helmut Schmidt, is no more prepared than Herr Strauss to accept reunification at the price of losing the security of the Western alliance.

Only the most extreme elements in the Social Democratic party (SPD) would happily embrace a modern version of the Rapacki Plan (a unified but 'neutral' Germany). Their relative weakness was demonstrated at the December 1979 annual conference, but they are strong among SPD youth; and if Ostpolitik and détente represent a 20-30 years' policy, the SPD's young Marxists may yet pose a serious threat to Western unity. Even now, left-wing leaders such as Herbert Wehner and Egon Bahr seek a weakening of the American link leading ultimately to a West German withdrawal from NATO in exchange for an undefined liberalization in the East and a united socialist commonwealth of Germany.

The dynamics of the German question weaken the alliance and distort West European politics; but it should be borne in mind that West German policy was devised in the light of Soviet pressures and American policy changes of the 1950s. Should the United States re-enter the Cold War waged by the Soviet Union, with all the damage to current reunification strategy that would entail, Bonn will brace itself and support America stoutly. After all, in Germany's case, the nation must survive to unite.

The West German response to President Carter's demand for support in oil-rich Southwest Asia proves the point. West Germans could have reasonably pointed out that, with 17 million German hostages the other side of the Iron Curtain, they could hardly be expected to feel too strongly about 50 American hostages in Iran. That they did not do so, but took a leading role in rallying support for sanctions against Iran and a boycott of the Moscow Olympics, indicates that Bonn does not hesitate to choose between Ostpolitik and the alliance when required by strong American leadership. Indeed, the West German Chancellor rose to this occasion despite having been badly embarrassed not long before when he agreed to have neutron bombs on German soil in the face of stormy opposition from his party only for the American President then to withdraw the request and cancel the project without notice.

The major immediate threat to security in West Germany is less the left-wing activists in the SPD than espionage and subversion directed by the Soviet Union and facilitated by the convenient agency of its East German satellite. In the other large countries of Western Europe, however, homegrown totalitarians flourish and gnaw away at traditional and popular national values and institutions, encouraged and in some cases assisted by Moscow.

In Italy, the largest Communist party (PCI) outside the

Eastern block is the official opposition in a basically two-party system. The extent of its independence from Moscow is questionable. Although it may disagree with or even attack specific Soviet actions, it would never regard the Soviet Union as an enemy nor support any destabilization of the Soviet dictatorships, as the PCI leader, Sgr Berlinguer, made clear during his 1980 visit to China.

Despite its defeat in the 1979 national elections, the PCI continues to contribute to Italy's inflation rate and political instability through its operation of the many large city and local governmental administrations it controls. At the same time, it contrives to evade any public responsibility for the nation's problems. It may be that national power will only interest Sgr Berlinguer's colleagues if and when the Christian Democrats are completely discredited and the country's economic and political institutions have collapsed. The possibility that the PCI's loss of support in the 1979 elections merely represents the emergence of increasing numbers of floating voters in Italy raises the spectre of the PCI gaining power in the next or subsequent elections by virtue of wider swings in the new political pendulum. In a curious twist of nationalist feeling, non-communists who feel a PCI government need not be mortal to Italian democracy or loyalty to the West allege that anti-authoritarianism and an instinctive capitalism in the Italian national character would successfully resist the apparatus of the communist state.

The French Communist party (PCF) pursues a strategy broadly similar to the PCI's but uses vastly different tactics in accordance with French circumstances. Unlike its Italian comrades, the PCF has a large rival Socialist party (PSF) to contend with. In conjunction with sympathetic Marxists in the PSF, the PCF has apparently succeeded in permanently divorcing its socialist rival from centrist politics and alliances, thus improving its own position and increasing its influence on the Left. It extends the spectrum, along which the PSF may be drawn further to the Left, by striking a much more openly pro-Soviet posture than its Italian counterpart. Significant changes leftward in PSF membership and official personnel have no doubt contributed to the transformation of French socialism, but how much of this change can be attributed to organized communist infiltration is difficult to assess.

The PCF-PSF Common Programme, the Union of the Left and its (temporary?) destruction by the PCF before the 1978 elections may be viewed as the sort of tactical manoeuvring by which the PCF may eventually destroy the PSF as a significant, independent and democratic party and also avoid embroilment in the politics of government until it is certain it can rule alone. Possibly the principal reason why the social democratic wing of the PSF is unable to reverse the party's leftward movement is that PSF candidates need communist votes to get elected. Also, the French Communist party and Marxist socialism in general have derived moral strength and reputability from détente, particularly as practised by the French government.

Enjoying the luxury of American protection at virtually no cost, and buffered against the Soviet world by West Germany, French diplomats belittle the United States and flirt with the Soviet Union in the cause of French 'independence'. France weakens NATO and seeks to manipulate the EEC and her allies to establish a special position between the two superpowers without recognizing that it is the tolerant and generous attitude of just one of those superpowers which alone enables her to indulge her fancies.

Curiously, in striving to assert French cultural and political nationalism at the expense of 'les Anglo-Saxons', right-wing and centre politicians in France have strengthened their Marxist political opponents by treating the Soviets as a civilized respectable regime legitimately representative of the Russian and subject peoples. Intellectual opinion on the boulevards of Paris may be deserting Marxism for a 'new conservatism', but this movement has as yet no counterpart in the political establishment, nor has it yet affected the parties of the Left.

Concessions to her allies are wrung from France only when America, Germany and Britain are sufficiently single-minded and determined to threaten to act without her, effectively facing her with isolation. Her speedy agreement to sanctions against Iran in April 1980, which surprised many commentators, may well have resulted from such a situation. Two weeks later, however, when the allies kept their ambassadors away from the Soviet May Day parade in Moscow, the French ambassador was pointedly there.

The Marxist capture of the French Left and the scandals and corruption shaking the political establishment are not good omens for the future of an already unreliable ally.

Across the Channel, the Marxist Left in Britain have destroyed the Labour party as a representative voice of democratic opinion, and détente helped smooth the way for them. The hard-line elements of Labour's left wing, including those favourable to the Soviet Union, control the party organization. They dominate the Trades Union Congress and the party's annual conference and National Executive Committee.

Aleksandr Shelepin and Boris Ponomarev have visited Britain as their honoured guests. They established formal friendly relations between the Labour party and the Communist parties of Eastern Europe. The 1917 Bolshevik revolution overthrew a social democratic government and destroyed a democratically elected Parliament, but Labour's NEC sent an official representative to the Soviet Communist party's sixtieth anniversary celebrations of the revolution. They appointed a Trotskyist militant as national youth officer of the Labour party. They promoted and protected militant extremists operating in the constituencies while they disciplined and even expelled moderates who fought back.

It is ironic to recall that barely a generation ago George Orwell openly attacked a Labour MP as a 'crypto-Communist' and Hugh Gaitskell asserted that a proportion of delegates at the 1952 Labour annual conference were 'Communists or Communist inspired'. At Scarborough in 1960, Gaitskell declared he would 'fight and fight and fight again' against 'fellow-travellers' amongst others demanding unilateral nuclear disarmament. Today, with the extremist problem ten or even a thousand times worse, Labour has no senior intellectual or political leaders of Orwellian or Gaitskellite character prepared to speak out so clearly and honestly. The silence of the parliamentary leadership signals the power of the Left.

Today, unilateral nuclear disarmament is official Labour party policy and the extremist party organization is less than ten seats away from controlling the parliamentary Labour party from within. A 'Great Purge' of moderates, inaugurated at the party's 1980 annual conference, will shortly deliver the PLP into the hands of the extreme left. This will lead ineluctably to extremist control of the Parliamentary leadership and the party election manifesto.

Labour MPs can, and do, rise in the House of Commons to defend the Soviet invasion of Afghanistan and Iranian militants holding American diplomats hostage. Opposition to sanctions in support of the United States was widespread in the PLP and left the leader, Mr Callaghan, virtually isolated in his own shadow Cabinet. Opposition to a boycott of the Moscow Olympics was official Labour policy and was featured in a major party campaign. Labour's 'alternative' economic policy would begin Britain's withdrawal from the Western trading system. It is now commonplace to point out that the Labour party programme is more left-wing than the manifesto of the Italian Communist party.

The implementation of present Labour policies, confirmed at the 1980 Blackpool Conference, would be the first steps in the removal of Britain from NATO. For instance, NATO becomes a liability to a Britain without her own nuclear deterrent. As a NATO base without nuclear capacity she would be exposed to nuclear devastation by Soviet forces as an expendable territory apart from the main area of conquest but still crucial to its defence and exceedingly difficult to invade and occupy, and therefore best eliminated. Also, if Britain abandons her own nuclear arsenal, it is unlikely that any NATO nuclear capability would be permitted to operate from British territory. Labour party policy would rule this out in any case.

Britain is the keystone of the alliance, the 'offshore aircraft carrier' which secures NATO's northern flank and is the crucial strategic base for the supply of an embattled Western Europe or eventual re-entry of allied power to an occupied Europe. If Italy or even France or Germany joined the Soviet orbit or were neutralized, it would be a critical blow to the remaining allies; but a Britain friendly to Moscow and divorced from Washington would render NATO and the defence of Western Europe unviable. Without Britain, the 'Finlandization' of the West would proceed apace.

Unlike the French and Italian Communist parties, the British Labour party is acknowledged as a party of government which has held office for half the post-war years. Despite Labour's recent mutation, the pendulum of British politics could reasonably be expected to return the party to power. The consequences of such an eventuality for Britain and the Western alliance are incalculable. Steps are being taken to forge a new centre party in Britain which can provide a democratic alternative to the Conservatives and represent, among others, the disfranchised traditional Labour voter; but they are only steps and are still at an early stage. More immediately helpful during 1980 in combating Marxist influences were the tangible discrediting of much of recent détente policy and the renewed determination of a spiritually revived United States to exert its influence in the world.

For some time American foreign policy has been characterized by weakness and vacillation, a lack of resolve perhaps reflecting, as former President Nixon has suggested, 'a weariness after nearly 40 years of bearing the burdens of world leadership'. Thirty years ago, the Korean experience showed that American democracy had a very limited taste for sustaining the blood costs of world policing. Vietnam confirmed this as well as America's unrivalled and admirable altruism, but it showed something else as well: that the Soviet Union knows how to take advantage of this altruism to divert America's energies from her most important interests.

The United States has always had a fascination for the Far East out of proportion to her real interests there. At the turn of the century, Theodore Roosevelt sought an American sphere of influence in China, but he understood that the open door most vital to the American economy and American security was in Europe. He gave it his highest priority and was central to the solution of the 1906 European crisis at Algeciras. His successors were less knowledgeable and less interested and consequently less able to influence events eight years later.

Europe is still the key to American security for the same geopolitical reasons. The United States today can less afford an unfriendly power in control of the West European peninsula than could Imperial Britain in the past. These physical facts are complemented by the less tangible facts of cultural and historical affinity which are more real than the universalist conceptions of some

Americans and Europeans. Those countries which share the values of Western Civilization have a right to defend the interests which are essential to the survival of their world.

The abiding weakness of the European nations, the diversion of America's energies by Vietnam and her eventual demoralization by the war lowered the alliance's defence of its most vital interests. This gave impetus to the shift in West German diplomacy toward Ostpolitik. It confirmed the French in their independent defence and foreign policies. The possibility that the American guarantee to Europe might lose its credibility led to the development of optional alternatives for national survival. Détente bought time and kept the United States involved, but it strengthened the Soviet Union and its subversive friends in Western Europe and increased the influence of those well-meaning people Lenin used to call his 'useful fools'.

Western interests require a strong American lead against Soviet expansionism and subversion. European nationalists, resentful former imperialists and *'bien-pensants'* may storm and complain bitterly, but Europe's democratic political leaders will always accede to determined American policies in areas of admitted mutual interest in and outside Europe. Although they know that America must defend them for the sake of her security, they also have to recognize that their own security is more at risk than hers and will have to make a commensurate contribution to defending the alliance's interests beyond their own frontiers.

If Western Europe is not to be 'Finlandized' and America isolated, the United States must learn to ignore the unwarranted superciliousness, carping and quavering which too often emanates from the liberal establishments and foreign ministries of Europe, and push the alliance forward with renewed self-confidence and vigour.

Index

Aron, Raymond 11
Atlantic alliance *see* Western
    alliance; NATO
Attlee, Clement 15

Bahr, Egon 7, 13, 99, 152
Bauer, Max 93
Berlinguer, Enrico 57, 71-4, 154
Bevin, Ernest 6-7, 15
Brandt, Willy 93, 95-7, 99, 121
Britain 42, 156; class conflict 6, 10;
    democracy in 30-42, 43-4, 156;
    and European security 12, 157-8;
    foreign policy 15-17, 19, 27, 139,
    157-8; Left in 1-7, 9-10, 15-16,
    17-26, 30-3, 156-7; state
    intervention 8, 21-2, 26, 41-2;
    see also Communist Party of
    Great Britain; Labour Party,
    Britain; trade unions

Callaghan, James 16, 21-2, 157
CDU (Christian Democrats),
    West Germany 93-5, 98, 100
Centre d'Etudes et de Recherches
    Socialistes (CERES) 84-5, 88
Chapple, Frank 6
Christian Democratic Party (Italy)
    4, 44, 51, 53-4, 58, 60-2; and the
    PCI 63, 67, 69-70, 72-6, 79, 154
Communist Party of Great Britain 4
Convention des Institutions
    Républicaines (CIR), France 83, 85

Deferre, Gaston 83-5
democracy: in Britain 30-42, 43-4,
    156; crisis of 43, 45-7, 49, 62,
    135, 145-7; in Italy 43-6, 48-50,
    52, 54-9, 61-2, 68, 154;
    in Scandinavia 103, 105; in
    West Germany 43, 94
democratic socialist parties 3, 4-6, 8,
    18, 21, 94-5; *see also under*
    individual parties
Démocratie Socialiste (DS) 85
Denmark 106-10, 114, 115-18, 119;
    communists 104-5, 108; social
    democrats 101-2, 107-9, 116-17,
    120-3
Duffy, Terry 38

Eurocommunism 6, 137, 144-5; and
    British Labour 22-3; and France
    90-1; and Italy 45; and Sweden
    104, 110
European Economic Community 16,
    19, 21, 47, 141, 149-50, 155
Evans, Moss 37-8

Fédération de la Gauche Démocrate
    et Socialiste (FGDS) 83-4
Finland 104
France 149, 160; Left in 1-3, 81-5,
    86-92, 154-6; social democracy
    87-9, 155; state ownership 87; *see
    also* PCF; PSF; social democratic
    parties

Free Democratic Party, West
Germany 95

Gaitskell, Hugh 15-16, 157
de Gaulle, General 81-4, 125
Gerhardsen, Einar 113
Germany, West 93-100, 102, 139,
149, 150-3, 155-6, 160; democracy
in 43, 94; Left in 95-8; state
intervention 94; trade unions in 6;
see also CDU; Ostpolitik; SPD
Giscard d'Estaing, Valerie 84, 91
Glistrup, Mogens 106-8, 110
Gustafsson, Lars 111, 115

Italy 43-62, 139, 149; democracy in
43-6, 48-50, 52, 54-9, 61-2, 68, 75,
154; economic development 46-8,
53, 57; elections 1979 63-80, 154;
Left in 46, 50, 63, 66-70, 74,
130-1; social conflict 44, 48-9, 52,
57, 60, 79-80; state intervention 8,
53, 76-80; terrorism 44, 49, 53-6,
58-60; see also Christian
Democratic Party; PCI; PSDI; PSI;
Radicals

Jones, Jack 37
Jospin, Lionel 90
Jouhaux, Léon 6

Keynes, M. 12
Kriegel, Annie 13

Labour Party, Britain 1, 15-29;
defence policy 17-18, 20, 23,
157-8; democracy in 30-4, 38-9,
41-2; foreign policy 15-23, 157-8;
leadership of 15-16, 20-1, 23-7,
31-2, 157; Left in 15-24, 30-3, 39,
156-8; membership of 24-6, 28,
33-4; problems of 3, 5, 120; social
democracy 15-16, 22-3, 25-7, 42;
and Soviet Union 5, 21-3, 156-7;
and trade unions 6, 33-8, 41; and
USA 23, 157; see also neutralism;
socialism

Labour's Programme, 1976 18-20,
22-3
Lange, Peter 45
Laqueur, Walter 55-6
Lecanuet, Jean 84-5
Left 137, 139, 143, 145, 151; in
Britain 1-7, 9-10, 15-16, 17-26,
30-3, 156-7; in France 1-3, 81-5,
86-92, 154-6; history of 1-4; in
Italy 46, 50, 53, 66-70, 74; at
local level 5-7, 24-5; in
Scandinavia 103-4; 107, 110,
112-14, 119-23; and Soviet Unio
11-12; and totalitarianism 4, 6,
8-9, 30, 50, 68, 75-6, 91, 153; in
West Germany 95-8

Marchais, Georges 86, 91
Marx, Karl 9, 11, 12
Mitterrand, François 13, 83-8, 90-1
mixed economy, commitment to
22-3, 97, 123
Mollet, Guy 3, 81-4
Moro, Aldo 52, 58-9
MRP (Centrist Christian party,
France) 83-5, 87-8
Myrdal, Gunnar 112

NATO 7, 15-16, 18-19, 95, 99,
117-19, 134-5, 139-41, 143, 150,
152, 155, 157-8; see also
Western alliance
neutralism of British Labour 17-23
Norway 113-14, 116-18; Communis
Party 104, 113; Labour Party
101-2, 104, 113-14, 117, 120-2

Ostpolitik 95, 97, 99-100, 151-3, 16

Palme, Olof 112-13, 122
PCE (Spanish Communist Party) 4,
22, 90
PCF (French Communist Party) 4-7
22, 81-6, 88-92, 154-5, 158; see
also France
PCI (Italian Communist Party) 4-5,
22, 44, 48-53, 54, 57-62, 90, 121,

153-4, 157-8; and elections 1979
63-79, 154
Popper, Karl 39
PSDI (Italian Social Democratic
Party) 50-1, 54, 62, 68-9, 74
PSF (French Socialist Party) 3, 5, 7,
81-92, 154-5
PSI (Italian Socialist Party) 51, 58,
61-2, 68, 74

Radicals, Italian 54, 67-9, 74
Rocard, Michel 88-9, 91

Scandinavia 101-24; communist
parties 102, 104-5; political issues
114-19; social democratic parties
101-4, 107-14, 115-16, 120-4; see
also under individual countries
Scanlon, Hugh 38
Schmidt, Helmut 96, 98-9, 152-3
social democratic parties 144, 147;
Britain 15-16, 21-3, 25-7, 42;
France 87-9, 155; Italy 50, 68;
Scandinavia 101-7, 117, 120-1,
123-4; West Germany 7, 94-8;
see also under individual parties
socialism 145; in Britain 17-22; 25-7;
crisis of 2-5, 62; in France 3, 155;
in Italy 3-4, 51, 58, 61-2, 68-71,
74-5; in Scandinavia 4, 105-8,
112, 114-15, 117, 120; in USA
12-13; in West Germany 4, 98
Soviet Union 11-13; and communist
parties 71-2, 89-91, 104, 146-7,
153-5; and threat to Europe 13,
20, 117-19, 125, 135, 138-41,
143-5, 149, 150, 153, 158-60
Spain 3, 8; see also PCE
SPD (West German Social
Democrats) 4, 7, 21, 93-100, 101,
152-3; Godesberg Programme 4,

94-5, 100, 120; 'Grand Coalition'
94-5
state intervention policies 8, 20-2,
24, 41-2, 53, 76-80, 87, 94,
109-11, 113, 115, 123-4
Sweden 109, 110-13, 114, 116-19;
Communist Party 104, 110; Social
Democratic Party 101-2, 104,
110-13, 115, 117-18, 120-3

Thatcher, Margaret 10, 144
trade unions: British 4, 6, 26-7, 30,
156; and communist influence 4,
137, 145-7; democracy in 34-8;
French 86, 89; Italian 78; and
Labour Party 4, 33-8, 41-2; in
Scandinavia 109, 113, 116-17,
120, 122; in USA 13

United States of America 125-33,
134-42, 143-7; and Britain 15-18,
23, 157-8; foreign policy 13,
15, 130-3, 135-42, 143-7, 149-53,
158-60; and France 82, 88;
socialism in 12-13; state
intervention 13; and Scandinavia
112, 118; and West Germany 95,
150-3; and Western security 12,
14, 125, 133, 135-6, 138-42, 143,
147, 149-51, 155-6, 159-60

Wehner, Herbert 7, 99, 152
Western alliance 134-42, 148-60; and
Britain 15-17, 157-8; and Italy 62,
154; and Scandinavia 117; and
West Germany 94, 96, 99-100,
150-3; see also NATO
Wilson, Harold 16, 25
working class in Europe 11-12, 22,
73, 89, 101-3, 110, 113-14, 120-1